THE LAW OF ATTRACTION AND ISLAM

a guide for positive change

BINIMAD AL-ATEEQI

Copyright © 2017 by Abdulaziz Imad Al-Ateeqi.

All rights reserved. No part of this book may be used or reproduced by any means, graphic, electronic, or mechanical, including photocopying, recording, taping or by any information storage retrieval system without the written permission of the author except in the case of brief quotations embodied in critical articles and reviews.

Because of the dynamic nature of the Internet, any web addresses or links contained in this book may have changed since publication and may no longer be valid. The views expressed in this work are solely those of the author and do not necessarily reflect the views of the publisher, and the publisher hereby disclaims any responsibility for them.

ACKNOWLEDGMENTS

With Love and Gratitude to:
My Mother Iman, my Father Dr. Imad,
My Wife Eng. Shaikha, My Daughter Noor,
And my two Sons Bader, and Imad.
Thank you.

TABLE OF CONTENTS

Part One: The Secret 1
    Introduction 1
    The Secret (Video Summary) 3
    Assumptions And Conclusions 5

Part Two: Law Of Attraction 7
    Law of Attraction Building Blocks 7
    The Self-Fulfilling Prophecy 9
    The Mind Body Connection 12
    The Power Of Suggestion 12
    Healing 19
    Mind Healing 20
    Medicine 22
    Energy Healing 23
    General Conclusions 27

Part Three: Islamic Relevance To The Secret 29
    The Sun That Blinds 29
    Credibility And Integrity 30
    What Else? 32
    Scientific Miracles 35
    Part Three Conclusion 44

Part Four: Islam And The Secret 47
    The Islamic Perspective 48
    The Ultimate Law Of Change 59
    The Methods 61
    Decisions (Change And Choices) 67
    The Power Of Words Over Decisions 68
    Priming 73
    Gratefulness And Invocation 79
    Destiny, Freewill, And Invocation (Prayers) 82
    Before We Conclude 87

Part Five: Conclusion 92
    Relevant Quran And Hadith 94
    Relevant Quotes On The Prophet Mohammed's (pbuh) Character And Personality 100

PART ONE
THE SECRET

INTRODUCTION

As I am writing these words, it is 5:46 P.M. Wednesday and I have just finished watching a video titled The Secret (Byrne R. 2006). Both excited and disappointed, I nearly spilt my cup of hot coffee as I rushed to the computer to write you these words. I will be sharing with you the fact that the secret is not a secret at all. Within this video, I saw people who have discovered something great but fell short of connecting all the pieces and consequently they were only able to see part of the puzzle!

> *"This secret gives you everything you want: happiness, health, and wealth."*
> —Bob Proctor

> *"You can have, do, or be anything you want."*
> —Dr. Joe Vitale

> *"We can have whatever it is we chose. I don't care how big it is."*
> —John Assaraf

The three quotes above are the opening phrases from the video The Secret, and I am sure you agree with me that they are some rather great claims. Are they true? Some of you may have already begun to ask the question, "What is this big secret and what does Islam have to do with it?"

The main effort of this book can be divided into two parts. The first part aim to deepen your understanding of what are the building blocks (the mechanics) of this secret. You will also be amazed as I show you how others in the fields of NLP, hypnosis, psychology, self-improvement, and even martial arts have noticed this "secret" and spoken about it without really understanding it. All of these are topics I have had a keen interest in for well over a decade now. The second part explains what the Islamic perspective is on "The Secret" and show you why it is incomplete without it.

This book aims to give you what the ultimate truth is concerning *The Secret* and the better way to go about applying it to achieve change and success. Both the main effort and aim are topics that require a deeper understanding of the human decision-making process. Great emphasis will be placed on delivering to you a clearer understanding of the latest developments concerning how your decisions are being made and what factors are influencing how you make a decision. You must first, however, know what the secret is and understand it as it was presented to the public and how it is **thought** that you should go about using it.

I will now briefly tell you what this secret is, the way it was presented by the film *The Secret*. What follows is my personal understanding of not only what the film *says* the secret is but also what it *implies* through several methods of presentation, representation, and even some (perhaps unintentional) misrepresentation. Once you understand the general idea, we can then proceed to examine it in more detail before later seeing what Islam has to say about this "secret." Soon you will begin to clearly understand the ultimate truth(s).

THE SECRET (VIDEO SUMMARY)

The film *The Secret* starts with a rather dramatic introduction that presents the secret as something ancient, that it was kept and guarded closely, and perhaps even stolen at some point. The opening scene continues to say, "The SECRET WAS BURIED... COVETED... SUPPRESSED" and that it "WILL NEVER BE REVEALED TO THE PUBLIC." It is explained that the greatest people in history knew this secret. Then you are told in many words that basically you can have whatever it is you want. Bob Proctor now tells you, "*The secret is* **The Law of Attraction**." It is explained that everything that happens to you in life you are attracting to yourself by what you think and by the images you hold in your mind. "Thoughts become things," you hear Mike Dooley say as the video continues. Then it is explained that thoughts have frequencies and that they are sending out a "magnetic signal" that attracts things to you. "The law does not care whether you perceive something as good or bad or whether you want it or don't want it." Basically it does not matter whether you're complaining about how bad it is, are thankful for how good it is, or whether you're saying "no" or "yes." **Your thoughts are part of the creation pattern of things that will manifest in your life.**

Next, it is shown that there is a time buffer so that things do not manifest immediately, which I understood as a kind of a safety mechanism.

Your emotional guidance system is also very important so that you don't have to try and monitor every thought you have which could drive you crazy! You feel either good or bad; all other emotions fall into one of these categories. Now in a brilliantly timed sentence, you learn that "whatever it is you are feeling, is a perfect reflection of what is in the process of becoming." You are told that your feelings are what attract things to your life, that:

> **"What you THINK**
> **And what you FEEL**
> **And what MANIFESTS**
> **Is always a MATCH"**

It is explained that there is a three-step process (The Creative Process), and that your role in this is (1) to **ask** for what you want; several methods are presented. The universe will (2) **answer** by rearranging itself for you. Finally, you must (3) **receive**; that is further explained in detail. The list of the things you can do to start turning your life around starts with **Gratitude**, which "shifts your energy" (allows you to focus on what you do have, not what you don't have). After the mention of a *morning gratefulness routine*, it is stressed how important visualization is to getting what you want. The next most prominent issue discussed is self or mental healing. Basically, that means you can heal and cure disease by removing stress and focusing on thoughts of good health. Again, several examples are given to support this. The negative role of resistance is then presented. It is clearly shown that resistance achieves the opposite of what many people use it for because it focuses attention on what you are resisting and not what you want to happen. Rev. Dr. Michael Beckwith explains it like this: "Take your attention away from what you don't want and all the emotional charge around it, and place the attention on what you wish to experience."

Dr. Ben Johnson then explains that we are all connected, that basically everything starting from us as humans to the entire universe is made from energy. James Arthur Ray likens God and energy by comparing their descriptions. According to Ray, quantum physics describes that energy "...can never be created or destroyed, *always was, always has been, everything that ever existed always exists*, its moving into form through form and out of form." He then continues that a theologian would describe God as "always was and always has been, never can be created or destroyed, all that ever was, always will be, always moving into form, through form, and out of form." Now, you are told that we are all connected, that "it's" just one energy field. *"You are a source of energy, you are eternal beings, you are God force, you are that which you call God,"* says Esther Hicks.(?) Rev. Dr. Michael Beckwith continues with *"We could say that we are the image and likeness of God."* Neal Donald Walsh pushes further on by stating "There is no blackboard in the sky. The blackboard doesn't exist," and that "Your purpose is what you say it is, your mission is the mission you give yourself, your life will be what you create it as, and no one will stand in judgment of it now or ever."(?) (Byrne, 2006, The Secret).

ASSUMPTIONS AND CONCLUSIONS

Generally, I thought it was an excellent attempt to portray the "Law of Attraction." Obviously, I have not covered every detail in the film nor do I intend to. The main point was to ensure that you have a sound understanding of what the "secret" is as I understood it. Every effort was made to bring to you the main ideas. I am sure that by now, some of you would agree that instead of the Law of Attraction, they might as well have said that the secret is that we are God and that the Law of Attraction is our tool or method for "creating" things! It's a shame, too, because they have indeed "discovered" something beautiful, something you will come to understand as you continue to read the rest of this book. I will go through The Secret step by step as presented above, pausing at each step to examine each concept or idea with an Islamic lens. However, **at this stage, it is enough to simply point out that their final conclusions about our place in the universe took a horrifying plunge into the darkness of assumptions partly due to misinterpreted observations.**

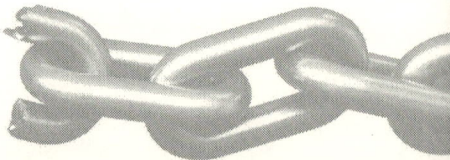

PART TWO
LAW OF ATTRACTION

LAW OF ATTRACTION BUILDING BLOCKS

Now before we move on to the Islamic perspective on all of this and what the **ultimate truth** is, let's see what else is there that is relevant to the subject at hand in the fields of NLP (neuro-linguistic programming), hypnosis, as well as other self improvement topics, and even martial arts. You will come to realize that many others have noticed this Law of Attraction in their own way and even spoke or wrote about it. Whether they referred to it directly or indirectly depended on their level of awareness and understanding. At an individual level nothing exists without awareness. If you are unaware of something then to you it simply does not and cannot exist. Even simply just "being" requires a level of consciousness. I do believe that something along these lines must have been on Rene Descartes' mind when he came up with his statement, "I think therefore I am." Jumping back on track, let us now see what others have noticed or discovered, whether recent or old concerning this matter.

In his book, *Awaken the Giant Within*, Anthony Robbins (2003) describes the five elements that make up the internal system for making decisions. He said that it acts like an "**invisible force**," (p.41: notice the similarity in terminology). He further explains that "by changing any one of these five elements—whether it's a core belief or rule, a value, a preference, a question, or an emotional state—you can immediately produce a powerful and measurable change in your life" (p.42). Again, you can see here that this focuses on your thoughts and emotions. Remember how *The Secret* focused on thoughts and emotions? Very interestingly, in this same book, Robbins (2003) later states that "Although we'd like to believe it's our intellect that really drives us, in most cases our *emotions*—the sensations that we link to our thoughts—are what truly drive us" (p.61). Yes, the word "emotions" is actually emphasized in the original text! No, the ultimate truth is not emotions. Just relax; you don't have to feel compelled and excited to learn and understand all this right now, because later on, the bigger picture becomes really clear. One more example from the master of self-development before we move on, and this one, like the others, is an important piece of this puzzle. Here, Robbins (2003) really drives home the concept when he says "We're not driven by reality, but by our perception of reality" (p.66). Again, you can see this persistent theme that points to the fact that what goes on inside you is more important than the events outside, that **your thoughts and emotions are of greater value and influence in your life than the reality that you live in**.

In his book *How to Hypnotize Anyone without Getting Caught*, Nathan Blaszak (2006) describes a method in which one simply imagines in detail what he would like and then it happens. He actually asks himself "Did I create this?" (p.118), then comments that "Your thoughts create your reality: What you can think, you can have, be, do, or experience" (p.118). He also goes on to use the term energy to describe this. Yes, in this book he does refer to the Law of Attraction as well. However, he does not go as far as to assume that we all may be little God fragments.

THE SELF-FULFILLING PROPHECY

After reading more on this topic which has gained so much publicity, I suddenly realized that in different terminology, this was a topic I am very familiar with. Three words suddenly materialized in my mind, "**Self-Fulfilling Prophecy.**" Basically, a Self-Fulfilling Prophecy is **a prediction that, in being made, actually causes itself to become true**. Can you see the relationship between this "prophecy" and the Law of Attraction? Need I go into the details of how a prediction is a thought? While both the Law of Attraction and the Self-Fulfilling Prophecy have spiritual and practical implications, the prophecy tends to lean more towards the practical nature of life and the psychological structure of human beings. For example, if you "believe" that all friendships end with fights, then it is inevitable that you will behave accordingly in your relationships. You will be projecting unconscious signals such as body language and "voice tones" that result in fulfilling that belief (by resulting in a fight within which you will be compelled to end the relationship based upon your preconceived belief). In the book *How to Read a Person Like a Book* by Gerard I. Nierenberg and Henry H. Calero (1994), it is pointed out that Freud had written, "The unconscious of one human being can react upon that of another without passing through the conscious" (p.6). Nathan Blaszak (2004) points this out statistically in the following manner: "Studies show that 90 percent of what you communicate with others isn't coming out of your mouth". That your tone of voice accounts for 30 percent, your body language for 60 percent, and therefore what you are actually saying (the words) is only 10 percent of what is being received by others (Introduction page). Diana Beaver (2002) offers an even lesser percentage saying, "words on their own make up less than 10 percent of our communication" (p.69). Everyone has had the experience where they found that often they could "release" an opinion and convey a lot about their character without uttering a single word by simply having others notice their reactions to whatever subject is being discussed.

In her book *NLP for Lazy Learning*, Diana Beaver describes the following experiment:

In an experiment, schoolchildren were given an IQ test at the beginning of the school year. Afterwards, the researchers arbitrarily divided the children into two classes without looking at the results, telling the teachers confidentially that the children in class A were the more intelligent. I have no doubt that the teachers kept the secret, but because Class A's teacher believed that those children were the bright ones, she treated them as such; and of course, Class B's teacher had no expectations of the 'less intelligent' children, and treated them accordingly. At the end of the year, the children were given another IQ test. This time it was marked. The children in class A did far better than the children in class B did. They had picked up subconscious messages that their teachers were sending them about their expectations, and so they lived up to those expectations (p.42).

The point is that even unintentionally, the subconscious aspects of human interaction based upon a belief can lead to a self-fulfilling prophecy.

By now, you must have realized that both the Law of Attraction and the Self-Fulfilling Prophecy are working on the same two levels. Both not only use the attraction "theory" (the universe will realign itself to give you what you think and feel), but they also gain a lot of credibility by simply causing the individual to interact with his environment in a way that leads to what he or she desires or expects.

You will see how this Self-Fulfilling Prophecy seems to be playing a role in one form or the other in many differing aspects of human life. Just like many things in life, it may have a positive or a negative role depending on the situation and one's perspective on events.

Under the topic of anxiety disorders and the issue of "catastrophic misinterpretation," the Introductory Textbook *Abnormal and Clinical Psychology* by Paul Bennet describes a process related to panic disorder. You will notice how this process and chain of thoughts are related to the Self-Fulfilling Prophecy. Bennet (2006) explains that:

"Once an individual has developed a tendency to interpret bodily sensations catastrophically, two further processes contribute to the maintenance of panic disorder. First, because they are frightened of certain sensations, they become hypervigilant and repeatedly scan their body checking for them. This internal focus of attention results in them noticing sensations that most people would not be aware of. Once noticed, these are taken as further evidence of the presence of a serious physical or mental disorder. Second, safety behaviors, usually involving not entering a feared situation, or leaving it at the onset of symptoms, tend to maintain the individual's negative interpretations" (p.187).

Sadly, in this case "the prophecy's" role is that of confirming preset beliefs based on misinterpretation, that are of a negative influence on the individual.

You already know now that both the Law of Attraction and the Self-Fulfilling Prophecy have interlocking roots and grow from the same pot of brain/mind and social science discoveries. Later, you will read more on the attraction theory part when I reveal its true "secret." For now, know that your thoughts and emotions are the building blocks of the Law of Attraction.

So far, we have focused on the theory behind how our thoughts and beliefs can cause a change in our lives by influencing our behavior in a way that will alter our life experiences. Next, we will see more examples which will demonstrate this. We will do so by examining the mind body connection to focus on how thoughts and beliefs can and do have a direct influence on our health and physical well being.

THE MIND BODY CONNECTION

In order to clearly illustrate how powerful our mind's grip is on our physical bodies, I think it is best to turn to the field of hypnosis. There have been many good attempts throughout history to define hypnosis. The most common definition you will find for this rather mysterious and often misunderstood phenomenon is that "It is an artificially induced altered state of consciousness that is characterized by heightened suggestibility and receptivity to direction." Receptivity to direction is another way of saying receptivity to suggestion. Let us now see examples that illustrate this power of suggestion.

THE POWER OF SUGGESTION

The power of suggestion is a topic that is closely tied to hypnosis. Besides the formal definition of hypnosis given above, I believe that it is also a linguistic art that can only truly be mastered by those who are skilled in manipulating language while remaining sensitive to their subject's paradigm.[1] Since hypnosis relies heavily on heightening sug-

---

[1] A paradigm is a set of assumptions, concepts, values, and practices that constitutes a way of viewing reality. It's another way of referring to perception

gestibility in the subject (the person), it is only natural that it would offer the most extreme forms of the power of suggestion.

One clear example of how our minds can directly cause physical effects on our bodies can be found in Ormond Mcgill's book *Professional Stage Hypnotism*. Mcgill (1977) explained that:

A blister can be caused on sound and healthy skin by applying a postage stamp and suggesting that it is a strong mustard plaster. Posthypnotic experiments have been performed in which a key or coin has been placed upon the skin of a subject with the suggestion that five minutes after awakening, a blister will appear at the spot where the key or coin had been placed, and be of corresponding size and shape. The key or coin is then removed, and the subject awakened, having no conscious knowledge of the suggestion given, but at the appointed time the blister appears shaped as the object" (p.72). It is a fact that with your thoughts, **you can** use your mind's ability to control most parts of your body.

Furthermore, an extreme example is given by the previous source that truly demonstrates the power of suggestion. It is said that:

Suggestions can carry an amazing amount of influence; an incident is told of a college student who was killed by its power. At a fraternity initiation, he was blindfolded, and after the usual emotion arousing proceedings, was told that he was to have his head chopped off. His head was then placed on the block, and viciously the knife slashed into his neck. It was actually only a wet towel, but the victim died—of heart failure. His subconscious had accepted the idea that the knife was real, and when the cold towel descended it ended his life. (Mcgill, 1977, p.29)

It seems different people develop different levels of security filters on how much is accepted by the conscious mind. The reason I chose the term "accepted" and not "allowed" is due to the fact that almost everything, whether you are conscious of it or not, seems to find its way to your brain. Your brain is capable of processing billions of thoughts per second but only a tiny fraction of them are made of conscious thoughts that you are actually aware of. In the book *Practicing College Learning Strategies* by Carolyn H. Hopper (2007), it is stated, "Your short-term memory holds only five to seven bits of information" (p.70). You may walk into an office and casually "look" to "see" if it's occupied or not. Then when asked to describe in detail what you "saw," it is very likely that you will only remember a small percent of what is in there. You may recall that there were two desks, a mirror on the wall, and maybe a telephone. Even when pressed hard, you may come up with no other information. However, under hypnosis when bypassing your conscious mind, you most likely can give far more details, and possibly even accurately describe how many lights were in the room and how many pinned notes were on the wooden board that was in plain view on the wall! Your eyes "saw" those things, they were recorded somewhere in that mass of nerves in your head. Likewise, when looking for your car in a crowded parking lot, you will most likely only "notice" the cars that are of similar color and model as yours, while your mind would have recorded almost the entire scene from your viewpoint, including smells, sounds, and your general mood (feelings). This is because when you are looking for something, your mind sets up "filters" on other things that have no memory record of being connected to the subject at hand. Hopper (2007), in writing about memory principles, explains, "The brain prioritizes by meaning, value, and relevance" (p.75). **Whether you notice something consciously or not, your mind records it and your unconscious may eventually be influenced by it.** The advertising industry understands this and spends millions of dollars bombarding you with subliminal messages to influence your decision-making process. Politicians know and use this as well. **All day long, you are being subjected to all kinds of data that does affect you whether you like it or not!**

The good news is that just by reading and understanding this, you have already heightened your sense of personal security. You may find yourself starting to "see" and "hear" how politicians, governments, news agencies, and all kinds of mainstream media are trying to "control" your freedom of choice. Again, you will notice that they all seem to concentrate on your emotions! Coincidence? Not a chance. They all understand another important fact, a fact which Dr. David J. Lieberman, clearly spells out in his book *Get Anyone to Do Anything*. The fact that *"Ninety percent of the decisions we make are based on emotion. We then use logic to justify our actions"* (Lieberman, 2000, p.62). Again, you see the leading role your emotions play in the drama of your life. This is further supported by Martin Lindstrom (2008), a leading expert in marketing, who, while commenting on what drives people's decisions to buy, said, "Emotion is one of the most powerful forces in driving what we buy" (p.165). He, too, estimates that "Ninety percent of our consumer buying is unconscious" (Lindstrom, 2008, p.195).

Did the presidential candidates in the 2016, US elections focus on logic or emotions? Was fear not the main factor in both campaigns?

So far you have seen examples of the power of suggestion that focused on the level of the individual; later on, you will read some more. We also highlighted the role of emotions which we will continue to do as we progress. For now, however, let us see examples of this power of suggestion and its effects on groups.

As with individuals, it is easy to find many examples on the power of suggestion that demonstrate how dramatic some of its effects can be on groups. Remember that in groups suggestibility also harnesses the power of peer pressure. Here is an incident I read about that was being used to describe the social factors that may be involved in developing conversion disorder:[2]

The condition has been described as contagious, in that the sight or knowledge of one person with unexplained symptoms may trigger similar symptoms in others, particularly in situations where people are grouped together and placed under some form of stress. One such incident among US army recruits was reported by Struewing and Gray (1990). They referred to the process as an epidemic, which occurred over a twelve-hour period following evacuation of 1800 men from their barracks owing to a suspected toxic gas exposure that turned out to be a false alarm. Despite the lack of toxin in the atmosphere, over two-thirds of the recruits developed at least one respiratory symptom, and 375 were evacuated by air ambulance for immediate medical investigation; 8 were kept in hospital. Two weeks after the incident, 55 percent of a sample of this group reported developing at least one symptom, including cough, light-headedness, chest pain, shortness of breath, headache, sore throat, or dizziness. (Bennet, 2006, p.133)

> Would it be possible for people in power with similar interests and goals to *manipulate* or "control" the general public, to **herd** YOU along with the masses unconsciously in ways that better serve their own agenda(s)? To achieve this, would they HAVE to *directly* **control** the media? Would you even be aware of it? What might their hidden intentions be?

The effect of thoughts on the physical body has been studied and used in many physical activities such as sports and martial arts. Here is how Dr. John M. La Tourrete (1998) sports psychologist and a

---

[2] Having various types neurologic symptoms that are not explained by standard medical evaluation.

tenth-degree degree black belt explains positive thought versus negative thought to students in his live two-hour seminar video titled *Beginner's Secrets to Poison Hands and Nerve Strikes*. A subject (martial artist) is asked to firmly outstretch his arm to the side. Now, La Tourrete tells him to say aloud "I am strong" as an attempt is made to force down the subject's arm and it is shown that it is firm and "strongly" held in place. Then, he (La Tourrete) asks the same subject to say in the same strong tone of voice "I'm not weak" which immediately causes his arm to be easily forced down. "He did hypnotic programming to himself," explains Dr. La Tourrete. The moment he even began to **think** the **words**, it directly affected his body. It is then further demonstrated that by saying "I'm not strong," the subject still maintains power in his arm; Dr. Tourrete sarcastically says, "I love those guys who say I'm not sick!" (La Tourrete, 1998).

It is as explained in the film *The Secret*, that it does not matter whether you are saying no to it or yes, it is what you focus on that matters! This demonstration highlights two topics discussed in *The Secret*.

First, it reconfirms the important role thoughts play in your life. Second, it highlights that you should not focus on what you don't want, but what you do want; remember that resistance achieves the opposite of what many people use it for, simply because it focuses attention on what you are resisting and not what you want to happen. This demonstration is saying exactly what Hale Dwoskin said in the video, which was basically that if you are against or anti something, be pro the opposite or what you want. My take on the subject is **Do not be anti "x," simply be pro "y."** Do not say, "I'm not weak," say, "I'm strong"; or at least "I'm not strong" if in fact you are physically or mentally "less than powerful." Have fun with this; I am not asking that you live a lie; Just be creative and have a positive perspective.

It is irrelevant whether an issue is getting positive or negative energy, both contribute to strengthening its existence. This is further confirmed by Lindstrom (2008), as he shared his finding by saying, "Explicit antismoking messages did more to encourage smoking than any deliberate campaign Marlboro or Camel could have come up with" (p.82).

Going back to the martial arts example, I would like to further add that martial arts also use self-directed suggestion in the form of visualization to get in to the right "mindset" in order to enhance performance. Often, this is accomplished by imagining the successful execution of certain movements.

In any advanced combat oriented training, no matter how skilled or tough you physically are, it simply does not matter how long you have trained if you do not have the proper mental frame of mind. Bruce Lee, who was the greatest martial artist of his time, understood the vital role that thoughts and emotions played in almost every part of one's life and in their ability to achieve their goals. In his book *Tao of Jeet Kune Do*, under the subject of training, he actually complains that:

"Too much time is given to the development of skill and too little to the development of the individual for participation. Training deals not with an object, but with the *human spirit* and *human emotions*" (Lee, 1975, p.27).

Yes, the word "emotions" is in italic in the original text. Later in the book, Lee emphasizes the importance of "the state of the athlete's mind" (p.68). You may be feeling now that on some level, you had known some of what was pointed out so far, yet you may be amazed that you did not notice it.

I know this from experience, too. In my over nine years of background in the martial arts, I've seen many who were amazingly skilled, yet were easily overpowered by opponents with poorer physical skills who were stronger mentally.

Previously, you may have noticed that the words "**think**" and "**words**" are in bold text. It may be appropriate here to note that your thoughts, often "one" with your emotions, are based on perception, and that the true power of all thoughts lies within the **words** you use to make up those thoughts. Most NLP (neuro- linguistic programming) books are quick to point this out. For those of you who may be unfamiliar with NLP, Beaver (2002) clarifies it in this manner:

"NLP has been described as the study of the structure of subjective experience: how or the way we process our thoughts affects our internal experience; how our internal experience affects our behavior; and how our behavior affects everyone else" (p.x).

Remember, you already realize something that connects this with the secret. That our internal experience affects not only our behavior but directly "sets up" our future. True? Yes and no. Later, you will see the whole picture. You can allow yourself, after completely reading this book, to "see" the world and your life under a brighter light, then you'll notice how good it feels to have more control.

HEALING

So far, I have shown you how what goes on in your head and what you feel directly affect your body. You also now understand that your emotions play a major role in the way your life unfolds. You can now start to see how powerful the connection is between your mind and body, and how greatly it affects your future. We will now deepen our understanding by going through how others are using these connections to achieve amazing results in "healing."

Having read this far, it should be of no surprise to you that your mind can achieve the miraculous in the field of healing. One of the great subtopics of this field is psychotherapy. Dr. George Weinberg (1996) says in his book *The Heart of Psychotherapy* that: "The aim of therapy is to help the patient cure himself" (p.16).

I thought it important to state this right from the start. I liked that the video *The Secret* actually puts the blame on the individual. It claims that everything that has happened to you, you attracted it to yourself. While not completely true it does seem to be generally the case. The truth is that at a very early stage in life, we learn to blame other people for what we perceive as negative events. This one false conclusion that we can avoid suffering by blaming others has caused many people far more pain than the anticipated pain of taking responsibility for our actions. In order to develop one's self, one must first change what it is that's causing the problem (usually a behavior based on some unconscious belief). However, once you have placed that responsibility on someone or something else, you have "freed" yourself from having to change, but certainly not from the problem. Like all new sciences, psychotherapy naturally was destined to be full of mistakes, but in doing so, it was able to develop as a science and art to the point where we all now can benefit from its findings. After all this history of research in to the human psyche, it settled down and found its place as a "tool" to help people **cure themselves**.

So according to psychotherapy, the mind has a "curing" capability. Does this only apply to the emotional, mental, and behavioral realm of our existence? You will now see that the answer is a firm no.

MIND HEALING

In an example from the video *The Secret*, it is shown how Cathy Goodman, who was diagnosed with breast cancer, says that she believed in her heart that she was already healed. She would say all day long "Thank you for my healing...on and on and on I went, thank you for my healing." She saw herself as if the cancer was never in her body. Other things she did were to avoid all stress and watch funny movies so that she would laugh a lot. It took approximately three months from the time she was diagnosed with cancer until she was healed, "and that's without radiation and chemotherapy," she points out.

Paul Bennet (2006), in his book *Abnormal and Clinical Psychology* says, "There is good evidence that stress can influence activity within the immune system" (p.386). Dr. John Hagelin explains within *The Secret* video, "happier thoughts lead essentially to a happier biochemistry and a happier healthier body; negative thoughts and stress are shown to seriously degrade the body and the function of the brain." So is Cathy Goodman's case some freak incident? Not at all, and I am going to show you more in order to further strengthen this belief in you so that you can truly benefit from this practice. Naturally, I will go into further detail later on so that you can see the "real" source of all this.

There are many study cases that clearly show how the mind can actually alter the body's biochemistry. Two of the best examples available are as follows:

First, it was noticed in research of people who have multiple personality disorders that "Incredibly, the potency of these people's beliefs that they had become a different person resulted in an unquestioned command to their nervous system to make measurable changes in their biochemistry. The result? Their bodies would literally transform before the researchers' eyes and begin to reflect a new identity at a moment's notice. Studies document such remarkable occurrences as patients' eye color actually changing as their personality changes, or physical marks disappearing and reappearing! Even diseases such as diabetes or high blood pressure come and go depending on the person's belief as to which personality they're manifesting" (Robbins, 2003, p.76).

The other case proves that the mind can actually override normal chemical reactions and this is clearly demonstrated in the ground-breaking experiment stated below:

"100 medical students were asked to participate in testing two new drugs. One was described to them as a super-stimulant in a red capsule, the other as a super-tranquilizer in a blue capsule. Unbeknownst to the students, the contents of the capsules had been switched: the red capsule was actually a barbiturate, and the blue capsule was actually an amphetamine. Yet half of the students developed physical reactions that went along with their expectations—exactly the opposite of the chemical reaction the drugs should have produced in their bodies! These students were not given placebos; they were given actual drugs, but their beliefs overrode the chemical impact of the drug on their bodies" (Robbins, 2003, p.76–77).

The mind can actually change the body's biochemistry based upon what you believe! Well, what other ways are there for healing to take place?

MEDICINE

We know that in general terms, medicine works by either replacing something that was missing or not functioning, or by altering cell activity, or by getting rid of infectious organisms and/or abnormal cells. It is a very effective method that has saved and bettered billions of lives. It being such a common method, I will not dwell on it, so let us move on. (The link between normal medication, mind healing, and energy healing will be examined further below.)

ENERGY HEALING

Energy healing is called by different names based upon different cultural interpretation. Most recently, these methods of healing are referred to as "arts." There are many arts that are essentially aimed at the same thing, though using different yet related methods for reaching the end result. Glenn Morris (1993) puts it this way in his book *Path Notes of an American Ninja Master*; "Rieki, medical chi kung, shiatsu, homeopathy, and therapeutic touch are all based on the principles of harmonizing the flow of life energy to speed or restore healing energy..." (p.122). He further adds, "Shiatsu, one of the Japanese massage therapies, is based on manipulation of the body's energy points and meridians, as is acupuncture" (p. 122). Basically, many non-western healing arts depend on manipulating bioenergy—or what is sometimes referred to by some as "chi" or "ki."[3] According to Michael Blake's (1983) book, *The Natural Healer's Acupressure Handbook—Basic G-Jo*, this energy is "thought to have a definite, predictable route through every body—to "flow" along a pathway that traverses the body in a fixed pattern somewhat like the network of a complex railway system" (p.xv). The book *The Ancient Art of Life and Death* by A. Flane Walker and Richard C. Bauer (2002) states that "According to Chinese theory, chi flows through the twelve primary meridians and two midline collaterals in a specific order" (p.29). This system was studied for both healing and combat. Practices like G-Jo use it for healing and first aid, while a Dim Mak (death strike) practitioner would use it to deliver...well...a death strike. Anyway, I can assure you that these arts are real even though some of the philosophy attached to it is false. Basically people may differ as to why being

---

[3] In China, it is called "Chi." In direct translation, it can mean "air" or "breathing." However, when it is taken further, it can mean "energy," "temper," "tension," or "endurance" (Cheung, 1996, under "Origins of Chi Exercises"). In the West, I have seen it called the "empty force" as in the book *Empty Force* by Paul Dong and Thomas Raffill

struck with a hammer is painful but rare is the one who will dispute that it is indeed painful. Modern research methods have now accumulated "...a considerable amount of archeological evidence to indicate medical arts flourished in ancient China up to 5,000 years ago" (Walker and Bauer, 2002, p.5).

Energy healing aims to manipulate energy flow within your body's natural pathways to the different organs in order to stimulate them to produce the electrochemical reactions that have historically been linked to ease or heal certain illnesses.

Energy effect on human and material bodies had been known in ancient times. Al-Kindi (801–873 AD), a well-known Arabic philosopher,[4] elaborated on the effects that stellar rays have and their alchemical applications. The Indians have long used colored stones to reflect stellar rays for therapeutic healing.

So now, you know that healing works in at least two other ways than just taking prescribed medicine. Very often, it is a mix of these methods.

1. Pharmaceutical medicines that interact with diseases and viruses (modern scientific way), and also the physical removal, alteration, or placement of organic and inorganic material in the body.

2. Your mind's ability to produce chemical alterations in the body and/or strengthen the immune system to combat sickness and speed up healing after injury (depends on your thoughts, beliefs, and emotions)

---

[4] For more information, read the book: *Al-Kindi the Father of Arab Philosophy* by Tony Abboud

3. Energy healing by manipulating energy flow in the body "along meridians or pathways of energy to and from each organ, stimulating them to produce electrochemical reactions"

You may have noticed that (2) is basically using your mind to accomplish what (3) does by external means. If the mind is too "weak" to utilize its "control" over bioenergy, then external methods of manipulation are required. By "external methods," I mean using needles or finger(s) on pressure points. Methods like the energy healing practices we have already covered.

Remember that even with conventional treatment methods using medicine, the effectiveness of doctor prescribed drugs' may be severely undermined if you do not believe in them. Your body may not fully utilize them as a tool to cure itself. Previously, I had shown you how thoughts and emotions affect the unfolding of your future; this will be further discussed later. Now you are realizing more than ever their direct effect on the body.

In the book *Social Psychology and Medicine* by M. Robin DiMatteo and Howard S. Friedman (1982), it is stated, "There is an enormous amount of evidence that thoughts and feelings are inextricably tied to physical process" (p.63). Let us examine this connection and the mental ability to heal starting with some examples from previous sources.

The first case is that of Norman Cousins, "the former editor of the Saturday review:

Cousins developed a degenerative disease that was progressively paralyzing him. His doctors told him that he had one chance in 500 of recovering. Cousins checked himself out of the hospital and into a hotel room. He devised his own treatment: laughter. He watched old

Candid Camera films and read humorous stories, and he recovered." (Byrne, 2006, The Secret)

Do you think he would have been cured if he did not believe in his ability to cure himself with the method he had chosen? Everyone knows at least one person or it may be you, who, at the mention of an illness, actually begin to "feel" the symptoms. How would someone like that react if they were in Norman's situation?

The second case is from the 1950s when medical researchers reported the discovery of a new drug called Krebiozen, which was believed to be a cure for cancer:

When the news was made public, a panic was created as thousands of cancer patients tried to obtain the drug, which was not generally available. Some patients did obtain it, and in many cases, the drug was dramatically effective. Some patients who were very ill and bedridden with cancer were given Krebiozen and soon were out of bed, their tumors shrinking miraculously. However, when later research showed that Krebiozen was ineffective, patients who had been helped with the drug suddenly had relapsed and died of their cancer" (DiMatteo and Friedman, 1982, p.60).

Okay, this one is not a happy ending, but the point is the fact that their tumors were actually shrinking when they "believed" that the drug worked!

At the risk of stopping prematurely, and as I am sure you are enjoying all this interesting complimentary information, what was presented is more than sufficient to accomplish what it was intended for. You will read more examples in this book that are also related to the mind body connection among other things. The fact is that if I were to attempt to gather all that is relevant, this book would surely not be completed in my lifetime. With the knowledge that you now possess, you can progress ever closer to the secrets of change, success, and the decision-making process that helps guide both.

GENERAL CONCLUSIONS

So what are the general (raw) results the previous body of literature may leads us to believe? Before deeper analysis they are:

1. That whatever situation you find your life to be in will not change until you change what's within yourself (thoughts, emotions...).

2. That there is a "Law of Attraction" that responds to what you ask and give you everything you want.

3. That there is an unknown time factor between asking for what you want and having it "manifest." Be patient and have faith because what you have asked for might be just underneath the surface and almost ready to "manifest."

4. That you should have a "morning gratefulness routine" because gratitude "shifts your energy" (allows you to focus on what you do have, not what you don't have).

5. That it is you who is attracting all those "negative" events in your life.

6. That you are a miraculous being with the ability to use your mind, your heart (emotions), and your senses to seek all that you desire.

7. That everything there is always was. That we are some sort of mini gods who can create things with our thoughts. That we can live however we want and we will never be judged. (?)

You will find the real truth concerning these seven conclusions and much more, right after you read the Islamic relevance section. For your benefit, I have made it a short and simple section that focuses on the general issues that are related to what you must know in relation to the topic at hand. Bear in mind It is not a summary of Islam, which would require volumes of books much thicker than this one.

PART THREE
ISLAMIC RELEVANCE TO THE SECRET

Because Islam is such a large subject, I will focus on those aspects that are of concern to the topic at hand. **This book does not aim to teach you Islam**. There are many others that you can go to if you are interested in knowing more. This book is designed to give you what the ultimate truth is concerning "the secret" and the better way to go about applying its components for change and success.

In order to address questions such as "What is Islam's perspective on the Law of Attraction" and "Is there an Islamic version of 'the secret?'" I have included this section to first answer questions like "I am not a Muslim, do I need to know this background information?" and "Why is it important?"

THE SUN THAT BLINDS

Whether you think you know Islam or are unfamiliar with Islam, it is critical for you now to read this quick background knowledge section in order to fully benefit from this book. This background information will allow us to smoothly progress to what this book is mainly about. Which of course is "What is Islam's perspective on the Law of Attraction?" This law that you now realize is actually a mix of many different, yet closely related topics.

While the title the "Law of Attraction" is a simple way to summarize a great deal of related issues, I do believe that it oversimplifies a complex matrix. **The risk is that this law becomes like the sun in midday: while the sun is by no means the biggest or brightest star in our sky, it does blind us from seeing the bigger and brighter stars. Our perceptions have been altered in such a way that many of us see the world from a limited perspective.** By the time you are done reading this book, you will see more and more how this tunnel vision syndrome seems to be blinding a great number of people.

CREDIBILITY AND INTEGRITY

Before we go into credibility, you should know that I would not be so selfish as to write all this so that only Muslims can benefit from it. It does not matter whether you are a Muslim or not, you may even be a hard-line atheist. You can allow yourself to approach this part from a purely scientific point of view if you choose to do so. Science and Islam have been best friends since day one. Nothing that was ever scientifically proven has ever been "un-Islamic." In fact, Islam has had a kind of confirmatory role in modern science. There have been many books that specialize in the scientific miracles of Islam. You will later be amazed to read some of the subjects that the Quran had described in detail at a time when it was absolutely impossible to know such things generally, let alone in detail.

Islam is sometimes referred to as an ocean (of knowledge) and that you should not attempt to dive in to it head first because you may drown. The Prophet Mohammed—peace be upon him (pbuh)—actually warned that anyone who may attempt to "take" Islam by force will be overpowered by it; meaning that if you approach it with extremism, it will defeat you. One of the most commonly emphasized teachings in Islam is "Choosing the middle way" and avoiding extremism because extremism destroys the person. The Prophet (pbuh) himself, whenever he would be given a choice between two things, would always choose that which was more lenient (easier), so long as it did not conflict with the teachings of Islam.

About the aforementioned the Prophet (pbuh) said, "The Religion is very easy and whoever overburdens himself in his religion it will overpower him. So you should not be extremists, but try to be near to perfection and receive the good tidings . . ."[5] and also in the authentic narration, "Never did Allah's Messenger (pbuh) make a choice between two things but adopting the easier one as compared to the difficult one, but his choice for the easier one was only in case it did not involve any sin, but if it involved sin he was the one who was the farthest from it amongst the people."[6]

Soon, you will find yourself reading what the Islamic perspective is on the secret. You will realize what the ultimate truth is, but in order for you to truly appreciate the knowledge I will share with you, you must first know the credibility of its source. Otherwise, it would be just my word against an ever- growing pool of opinions and guesses.

Credibility is basically the sum of components that give believability of a source or message. It includes, but is not limited to, trustworthiness and expertise. Soon, you will realize that the Quran easily surpasses all other books, whether religious or otherwise, with respect to credibility.

---

[5] Authentic narration from Sahih Al-Bukhari, number 39
[6] See the authentic narration in Sahih Muslim, number 2327.

The Quran's historic credibility is established by being completely memorized by millions of Muslims worldwide from the day of its revelation to this day. People who have memorized the Quran not only know it by heart, every letter of every word in every verse and their exact order; they also have memorized the exact pronunciation of every letter and word. Every Quran in the entire world is an exact copy of the original text. The Islamic community has always been very serious in its preservation of the Quran. In fact, if a single letter misprint occurs, immediately the books are collected and completely destroyed. Upon receiving the revelations from the angel Gabriel (AS), the Prophet Mohammed (pbuh), would recite the exact words he heard in their exact order, and then they would be memorized or written letter by letter by his companions. His companions and all Muslims would memorize them by heart after hearing the Prophet recite them. Many have written about this topic, going into great detail which I will spare you here in order to remain focused on the reason you purchased this book. So **the Quran is historically authentic** (i.e. not a single letter changed from its first revelation).

WHAT ELSE?

The Quran is scientifically flawless. I am not referring to the fact that it is **a miracle in its use of language**, or the fact that it is **numerically**[7] **a miracle**. I am referring to the fact that **many recent scientific discoveries made using the latest technology were already described in detail over fourteen centuries ago in the Quran**. It is important to remember that the Quran is not a science book. However, the matter of fact way in which it asks that you reflect

---

[7] Mathematicians have had a great interest in the numerical symmetry and other very interesting numerical "coincidences" related to mathematical calculations.

upon and ponder the magnificence of all that was created as it describes these "scientific" details is miraculous.

Keep in mind that the Quran was revealed over 1430 years ago and I need not tell you, as I am sure you can imagine the level of knowledge and what sorts of beliefs people had during that time. Second, the Prophet Mohammed (pbuh) was actually illiterate! He could not read or write, as he was uneducated. He was however "called" (nicknamed) by people in Mecca as "AlSadiq AlAmeen" which literally means "The honest, the trustworthy." Key to note here is that this title was held before he started calling for Islam. It is well documented that **his integrity was unquestionable**, to such an extent that even after he became a Prophet, those who became his most aggressive enemies would still leave their valuables with him for safekeeping when they traveled out of Mecca because he was the most trust worthy person they knew in a city full of very honest people and where dishonesty was a major taboo. Now, that is integrity![8]

One more thing to note here is that Islam is not just based on the teachings of the Quran; it is also based on the "hadith" (recorded sayings/actions of the Prophet pbuh) that collectively form the core of what is called "Sunna."[9] These also have been preserved with as much enthusiasm but are classified in varying degrees of authenticity: from

---

[8] Please see list of quotes by a variety of Eastern and Western thinkers and scholars, with respect to the character of the Prophet (pbuh). This I provide to offer an unbiased perspective by non-Muslim critics for those interested in a fast background check on this issue.

[9] Sunna basically means "the way" (of the prophet)that is based on all the authentically documented works with respect to all actions, sayings, comments, or the absence of (i.e silence or inaction), with respect to the life of the Prophet Mohammed (PBUH). It includes some obligatory but mostly recommended behavioral guidance for Muslims. The non-obligatory realm within it ranges from the highly recommended to the highly discouraged. Its status is second only to the holy Quran. For more details about understanding these issues look out for my forthcoming book: The Prophet Muhammad (PBUH), A Comprehensive and Contextual Biography.

the unquestionably authentic and trusted level, down to the weak and possibly altered or false level, and are preserved as just that. Lower classes of authenticity hadith are excluded from the decision-making cycle in Islam with regards to religious verdicts. Likewise, any Hadith you see in this book will be 100 percent authentic. There is no point in referencing something that may be of questionable accuracy in wording or meaning when you have available what is authentic (of undisputed accuracy, origin, and authorship). This authenticity remains usable for both believers and nonbelievers because it relates to the original writing of the text and not the concept of whether one believes the source to be a Prophet of God or not.

> Professor K. S. Ramakrishna Rao (1978), head of the Department of Philosophy, Government College for Women University of Mysore, Mandya (Karnatika, India) states that:
>
> "Even a hostile critic like Sir William Muir, speaking about the holy Quran says that, "There is probably in the world no other book which has remained twelve centuries with so pure a text." I may also add Prophet Mohammad is also a historic personality, every event of whose life had been most carefully recorded and even the minutest details preserved intact for posterity" (Ramakrishna Rao, 1978).
>
> A list of relevant quotes from Western and Eastern scholars and intellectuals with respect to the Prophet Mohammed (pbuh) is provided later in the book as further reference for those interested in knowing more about his character.

You will now see a few examples of Islam's scientific miracles, which I will present here only as samples to further highlight the point.

Credibility is of importance since we will be using Islam to examine what was previously mentioned and more. For non- Muslims if it is a perfectly accurate source for truth about what can be tested it is very useful to use it in checking other issues; regardless of what even an atheist may think of its origin.

SCIENTIFIC MIRACLES

The main category we are going to examine with respect to scientific miracles is our universe and some of the related topics. This category was chosen out of many and it makes the point which I will later state at the end of this section.

THE UNIVERSE AND RELATED TOPICS:

It is appropriate here to note that many Ayat (Quran verses) may have multiple levels of meaning embedded within but never contradicting and always enriching the meaning in ways that appeal to both layman and scientist. In fact the word Ayat (plural) or Aya (singular) actually means "verses" or/and "signs" or/and "miracles" or/and "proof." Yes—"or/and"—because depending on the context, it may mean all, some, or only one of those related meanings.

a. The Big Bang Theory and the Expansion of the Universe

In Islam, the history of creation goes as far back as to when there was nothing but God (Allah) The Almighty, and it details what the Most Merciful created first. This is beyond the reach of science at this date, and therefore we will begin with what we can grasp in light of where science has gone so far.

This dictates that we begin with Surat Al-Anbiya:

> *"Do not the unbelievers see that the heavens and earth were joined together (as one unit of creation) before we clove them asunder, and made from water every living thing? Then will they not believe."*
>
> Quran 21:30

This "Aya" states that the entire universe including the earth were once all joined together as one unit and then were forcefully pulled or pushed apart. It is also significant that this Aya is specifically addressed to nonbelievers, implying perhaps, that the unveiling of the secret mentioned in this Aya would be made by nonbelievers, as a sign for them. Was it a "nonbeliever" who made this discovery?

The conclusion that astrophysics has reached today is that the entire universe, together with the dimensions of matter and time, came into existence as a result of a great explosion that occurred in no time. This event, known as "The Big Bang," produced the entire universe about 10–15 billion years ago, creating it from nothingness as the result of the explosion of a single point. Modern scientific circles are in agreement that the Big Bang is the only rational and provable explanation for the beginning of the universe and of how the universe came into being. So scientists have now accepted the Big Bang theory as the answer to how the universe began. The theory states that the universe was initiated from a singularity that suddenly erupted, leading to the creation of the universe. Clearly, science and the Quran are in agreement here. The difference is that the Quran had stated it fourteen centuries ago.

This leads us right to this next Aya of interest:

"He is the Originator of the heavens and the earth...."

Quran 6:101

Here we have an Aya that says that there was at one point nothing. This is indicated by the use of the word "originator." So basically, this means that the universe and earth did not always exist, and that at some stage, there was no universe.

Through science, we now know that before the Big Bang, our universe did not exist in its current state. There was no such thing as matter. A condition of nonexistence in which neither matter, energy, nor even time, existed. As previously mentioned in other words, there was no universe before the Big Bang. This can only mean one thing. This is that matter, energy, and time were all created. The idea that the universe and earth did not always exist is a basic belief in Islam, and only very recently did scientists discover this.

Before moving on, I would like to look at one more Aya that is of relevance to the topic at hand.

"And it is we (Allah) who have constructed the heaven with might, and verily, it is we who are steadily expanding it."

Quran 51: 47

In this Aya, it is clearly said that the universe was constructed, and that it is expanding. Here we will focus on the declaration that the universe is expanding.

The universe IS expanding! Rarely will an astronomy book leave out this important detail of our universe. I will only give two examples of this to avoid flogging a dead horse on this matter. The first can be found in Craig J. Hogan's (1998) book *The Little Book of the Big Bang*, in which it is clearly stated that "The overall motion of the universe is expansion" (p.47). The second is in Stephen Hawking's (1998) book, *A*

Brief History of Time where he, too, clearly spells out that "The universe is expanding" (p.9). This concept of the expanding universe has been universally accepted by the scientific community as "fact." This discovery was first made by Edwin Hubble in the 1920s (Hawking, 1998, pp. 38-41). Then in 1929, further observations were published and are explained by Hawking (1998) in the following manner: "The farther a galaxy is, the faster it is moving away!... the universe could not be static, as everyone previously had thought,[10] but is in fact expanding; the distance between the different galaxies is growing all the time" (p.41).

It was impossible to know or observe this detail until only very recently. Was it possible for an illiterate man to have observed this expansion over fourteen centuries ago?

b. Clouds of Smoke and the Sky Full of Orbits

After the Big Bang, we have time, matter, and energy. Then what happened? How did the stars and planets come to be?

An Aya from the Quran reveals:

> *"Then he turned to heaven when it was smoke and said to it and to the earth, "Come [into being]..."*
>
> Quran 41:11

"Come" in this Aya literally means "come forth," or "become," or "do as commanded."

In this Aya, it is stated that the universe was once smoke. Then it was

---

10 Hawking here confirms that "everyone" previously had thought that the universe was "static." He was obviously unaware of this Aya.

formed into the galaxies and the earth, as we know them. Let's have a look at what science says about this:

In cosmology, it is now accepted that the universe was indeed a cloud of smoke before it formed galaxies. Looking at our solar system as an example, we can see that it was formed from an enormous rotating cloud called the solar nebula. According to Tarbuck and Lutgens (2002), five billion years ago, this huge cloud of gases and minute particles began to gravitationally contract. Due to this contraction, it rotated faster for the same reason ice skaters do when they draw their arms towards their bodies. Eventually, the inward pull of gravity came into balance with the outward force caused by the rotational motion of the nebula. By this time, the once vast cloud had assumed a flat disk shape with a large concentration of material at its center called the protosun (pre-sun). The formation of the sun marked the end of the contraction period. What remained now orbiting the sun would form our solar system's planets including Earth, in a few tens of millions of years (p.19–20).

Again, we see that as impossible as it sounds, the fact remains that what only very recently was discovered by science was already revealed in the Quran over fourteen centuries ago.

Now we have our solar system with the sun, planets, and moons among other things. Let us focus a bit on our Moon and the Sun. Reading the Quran, you will notice that it specifically and repeatedly describes the sun's light and the moons light using different words. Dr. Zaghlool Al-Najar (2001) explains that the Quran speaks of noor and dheyaa when describing the light emanating from the moon and sun. The moon's light being a noor and the Sun's light a dheyaa. Never does the Quran refer to the sun as a noor or the moon as a dheyaa. (Keep in mind that both translated mean "light.") The secret is that dheyaa specifically refers to an object that produces or is the source of its own light, while noor is reflected light! In this next Aya, the sun is described using a different word:

> *"Do you not consider how Allah has created seven skies in layers, and made the moon therein a noor (a reflected light) and made the sun a seraj (burning lamp)"*
>
> Quran 71:15–16

Dr. Al-Najar continues to say that "no one had known that the Sun is a "seraj" (i.e. like a burning lamp); its fuel is hydrogen gas." Only lately did scientists realize that the moon's light is only a reflection of the sun's light and that it (the moon) does not produce light (Al-Najar, 2001). Exact and specific detail presented in a matter-of-fact way that is scientifically shocking concerning the time period from when this was revealed (Over 1430 years ago!).

This appropriately leads us to this next group of verses:

> *"It is He who created the night and the day, and the sun and the moon. They swim along, each in an orbit."*
>
> Quran 21:33

> *"And the sun runs to its resting place. That is the decree of the Almighty, the All-Knowing."*
>
> Quran 36:38

> *"By the sky, full of paths and orbits."*[11]
>
> Quran 51: 7

In the above verses and many others in the Quran, it is emphasized

---

11 The Arabic word translated here as "paths and orbits," interestingly also incorporates within its meaning the "connectedness or attraction of bodies."

that both the sun and the moon **move in orbits**. Then it is further mentioned that the sun is moving towards a specific destiny where it will rest. Finally, it is declared that our entire universe is full of orbits. Our moon moves in an orbit, and our sun moves in an orbit, but also towards a specific place, and all this in a sky full of motion and other orbits.

Let us first consider the moon; we all know that it does in fact orbit the earth. When we look at modern astronomy books, we will find that the sun does indeed move in its own orbit called the Solar Apex. Furthermore, science has discovered that the sun is moving towards something in particular. It is moving at the enormous speed of 720,000 kilometers an hour towards the star Vega. Along with the sun, all planets and satellites within the gravitational system of the sun also travel the same distance. In addition, all the stars in the universe are in a similar planned motion. The following is how Stephen Hawking (2001) describes our galaxy in his book *A Brief History of Time*:

We live in a galaxy that is about one hundred thousand light-years across and is slowly rotating; the stars in its spiral arms orbit around its center about once every several hundred million years (p.39)." We now know that our galaxy is only one of some hundred thousand million that can be seen using modern telescopes, each galaxy itself containing some hundred thousand million stars (p.38).

Should I even bother restating that this was stated as a fact, not theory, over fourteen centuries ago? Without super telescopes or advanced observation technologies to observe space in a range of millions of miles, nor the modern knowledge of physics or astronomy!

Speaking of "observation," let us bring the following verse into the picture. In Surat al-Waqi'ah, The Creator swears by his creations in this manner:

"I swear by the locations of the stars, and indeed, it is a {most} great oath- if you know."

Quran 56: 75–76

Why swear by their locations and not the actual stars? You know that all we really "see" in the sky is the locations of stars. It takes so long for their light to actually reach the earth that what we actually see may be what WAS, millions of years ago. Stephen Hawking (1998) notes that, "The nearest star, called Proxima Centauri, is found to be about four light-years away (the light from it takes about four years to reach earth) or about twenty- three million million miles" (p.37). Knowing that the universe is in constant motion, you realize that what you are looking at may no longer exist or has completely changed its location. Specialists in this field will naturally have a deeper respect and appreciation for the "greatness" of this oath and why The Creator would swear by the location of his stars. They would understand the role of gravity in the universe and how the locations of great stars affect the order and movement of matter within space.

c. Sunrises and Sunsets

Dr. Al-Najar (2001) explains by starting with a recitation of Surat Luqman:

"Do you not see {i.e., know} that Allah causes the night to enter the day and causes the day to enter the night, and has subjected the sun and the moon, each running {its course} for a specified term, and that Allah, with whatever you do is Acquainted?"

Quran 31:29

He causes the night to enter the day and causes the day to enter the night"; night and day are not physical bodies—they are a state of the earth. At every time, you will find that about half the earth is in day and the other half in night. The earth moves and they alternate/exchange positions in a constant manner. We read in Surat Fatir:

> *"He causes the night to enter (pass/merge into) the day, and causes the day to enter the night and has subjected the sun and the moon—each running [its course] for a specified term. That is Allah, your Lord, to Him belongs sovereignty..."*
>
> Quran 35:13

Then in Surat al- Ma'arij:

> *"So I swear by the Lord of {all} risings and settings that indeed we are able"*
>
> Quran 70:40

What is strange is that we know the earth leans on its axis to cause the seasons, without which life would not sustain itself on earth. This leaning causes every point on earth to have a rising and setting time different from the others; and that these risings and settings have an end point—the furthest points east for rising or setting and the furthest points north and south. We find that the Quran speaks of "Lord of the sunset and sunrise", and "Lord of the two sunsets and Lord of the two sunrises" and "the Lord of the risings and settings". Uttermost accuracy: There is a sunrise (east) and a sunset (west) for every point on earth. There are two sunsets and two sunrises, the furthest point away north and south for sunrise, and the furthest point away south and north for sunset, and many sunsets and sunrises between those two ends. No one at the time of the Prophet (pbuh) had known this and not even many years after his time," (Al Najar, 2001). I would add regarding the many sunsets and sunrises that our sun shines on more than just our planet and that proves that indeed there are many sunrises and sunsets. Furthermore there are billions of stars in the universe and many of them are likely to also have held captive in their gravitational pull celestial bodies that also witness sunrise and sunset from that star according to their unique circumstances of rotational speed and other factors. So much more information is available under the general topic of the universe and our sky but this is not what this book is about.

> Although I would have liked to include many more references for what I had written concerning the universe and our sky, a lot of this is now common knowledge. The information here is basic to general education in high schools and universities. I thank, Dr. Zaghlol Al-Najar for the impressive effort he has put forth in the analysis and presentation of his findings and expertise in the field of Science and Islam. There are also many websites now in many languages that present this topic with greater detail.

PART THREE CONCLUSION

Is it just the universe and our sky that is miraculously detailed in the Quran?

Plants, animals, water, numerics, geology, astronomy, legislation, prophetic, anatomy, genealogy, embryology, history, medical... the list goes on! Not a single scientific contradiction or discrepancy! Detail after detail is casually described in a matter-of-fact manner that simply refers to them as examples of creation or what we can marvel at to witness the magnificence and miracle of creation. Very often, The All-Knowing, The Most Merciful specifically states that these are "Ayat" ("verses," "signs," "miracles," "proof") for those who are "scientists," "have awareness," "have knowledge," and "understanding."

An example of such Ayat is found in Surat Al-'Imran:

"Indeed, in the creation of the heavens and earth and the alteration of the night and day are signs for those of understanding who remember Allah while standing or sitting or {lying} on their sides and give thought to the creation of the heavens and the earth, {saying} "Our Lord, you did not create this aimlessly, exalted are You {above such a thing}, then protect us from the punishment of the fire."
Quran 3:190–191)

Indeed, The Lord can say be and it becomes so, but the All-Knowing has made it so that man, to whom he blessed with a brain, can "learn" and give praise to He who is in no need of such praise. The first Words the Most Merciful sent to his final Messenger and seal of prophets (pbuh) contained a key message to all of us: That the days of the Super miracles (i.e. like the ones given to Mosa (Moses) and Essa (Jesus) God's Peace be upon them both, are over. It was the beginning of the time of knowledge and science. So it was sent (the first Quran to be heard by humanity and the first words of the final message) Surah al- 'Alaq, Aya 1–8:

"Recite {read} in the name of your lord who created—created man from 'alaq (a clinging or suspended substance); recite {read} and your lord is Most Generous—who taught by the pen, taught man that which he knew not; No! {But} indeed man transgresses, because he sees him- self self-sufficient, indeed to your lord is the return."

We know now that 'alaq[12] is one of the stages the human embryo goes through in the uterus.

There is a book out there that has been continuously and accurately giving the truth about all kinds of life issues. So what? Well, this means that whether you are an atheist, Buddhist, Christian, Jewish, or Muslim; if in fact you do see yourself as even slightly logical, you should at least use it as a great mysterious source of accurate knowledge. Let us not forget that the miracles in Islam are not only found in the Quran but also in the sayings of the Prophet and his "Sunna." It is your personal choice to believe in The Most Merciful, The Creator or not, but surely with scientific evidence like this, it would be naïve not to use the Quran and Sunna knowledge to examine something you are about to invest so much time and effort into. It has never been incorrect since its existence, so why not examine what ultimate truth and light it can shed on the Law of Attraction?

---

[12] 'Alaq literally means three things: 1. leech, 2. suspended thing, 3. blood clot. During the 'Alaq stage, the embryo looks like a leech, and behaves like one by the means of which it obtains nourishment (feeding off the blood of others). Second, it fulfills the "suspended thing" definition because of the embryo's suspension during this stage in the mother's womb. Third, at this stage, we find that the external appearance of the embryo and its sac is similar to that of a blood clot; furthermore is that the blood in an embryo at this stage does not circulate. (blood circulates at the end of the third week) (A Brief Illustrated Guide to Understanding Islam, second edition by I.A. Ibrahim, pages 6–8)

PART FOUR
ISLAM AND THE SECRET

Finally, we are now ready to examine our findings from an Islamic point of view. We understand that Islam's perspective will be of great value due to its second-to-none record of accuracy in observing and stating the truth with respect to all that we may be able to examine and validate within the limits of scientific research.

Let's start by reviewing what has been concluded from the secret (the Law of Attraction). We will then see what the Islamic perspective is, and further build upon those findings with other Islamic or scientific backup. You may notice and feel your image of life maturing as the cover of darkness is lifted and your eyes begin to adjust to the light of ultimate truth. So what was concluded?

1. That whatever situation you find your life to be in will not change until you change what's within yourself (thoughts, emotions...). This is the basic principle behind the Law of Attraction.

2. That there is a "Law of Attraction" that responds to what

you ask, and it can give you everything you want. (You must ask for what you want.)

3. That there is an unknown time lapse between asking for what you want and having it "manifest." Be patient and have faith because what you have asked for might be just underneath the surface and almost ready to "manifest.

4. That you should have a "morning gratefulness routine" because gratitude "shifts your energy" (allows you to focus on what you do have, not what you don't have).

5. That it is you who is attracting all those "negative" events in your life. (what is negative in your life is your doing.)

6. That you are a miraculous being with the ability to use your mind, your heart (emotions), and your senses to seek all that you desire. Moreover, the universe is on your side: It will "arrange" it for you.

7. That according to *The Secret* everything there is always was. That people are some sort of mini gods who can create things with their thoughts. That we can live however we want and we will never be judged.

Let us examine these findings with the truth and fact lens of Islam.

THE ISLAMIC PERSPECTIVE

1. **Whatever situation you find your life to be in will not change until you change what's within yourself.** *This is the ultimate conclusion of several centuries of research into the human psyche, social studies, and life in general.* Now this

sounded very familiar to me. Then I realized I already knew this. I had read this in the Quran Surat Arra'd:

"...Indeed, Allah will not change the condition of a people until they change what is in themselves..."

Quran 3:11

Here is something Nathan Blaszak (2006) said, perhaps not realizing that he was actually rephrasing something that was known in Islam over fourteen centuries ago: "Change the way you're thinking on the inside, and the rest of the world changes, too" (p.13). Note that being a believer was not specified as a condition. So, no; you don't have to be a Muslim for this to work. He who has created you set **a LAW that your condition for changing has as a prerequisite in you changing what is within you!** (Your thoughts, emotions, and beliefs!) This is the ULTIMATE LAW. It is of importance to remember here that this addresses societies (people), and for your society to achieve this, it is mandatory that YOU do this. Individuals are the building blocks of society, and families are the units that if corrected, all of society WILL be corrected.

2. There is a "Law of Attraction" that responds to what you ask and it can give you everything you want (You must ask for what you want).

Allah the all mighty tells us in Surat Ibraheem:

"And he (Allah) gave you all you asked of him[13] and if you should count the favor {i.e., blessings} of Allah, you could

---

13 Something of what you asked and all of what you continually require according to his wisdom.

not enumerate them. Indeed, mankind is {generally} most unjust and disbelieving [un-grateful and denying of Allah's favor.]"

Quran 14:34

Key to note here is that this "giving of what you ask" is not just for the believers, as indicated by the last word in the Aya (disbelieving). It addresses all mankind. Good news for non- Muslims and anyone who chooses to limit their goals to this lifetime only. Realize that whether you believe in God or not, it is he who has blessed you with the freedom to do so, and in the end it is to God that all matters return.

In Surat Al-Baqarah, it is further explained and put in this manner:

"And when My servants ask you, {O Mohammed}, concerning me—indeed I am near, I respond to the invocation of the supplicant when he calls upon me. So let them respond to Me that they may be [rightly] guided."

Quran 2:186

So God says that He is close, responding to the prayers of those who ask. What other examples are there? The Most Merciful also prompts you to ask in this manner from Surat Ghafir:

"And your lord says "Call upon me {ask/pray}, I will respond to you...."

Quran 40:60

Knowing the Law of Attraction, you understand that it depends on your mind's ability to "connect with the universe" to reach out; that you send the signal for what you want. This is what they referred to as the first step, the step of asking for what you want—invocation (Prayer)! Weather ignorance or pride they seem to prefer asking the "universe" over asking God!

3. **There is an unknown time lapse between asking for what you want and having it "manifest." Be patient and have faith**. This is such a broad subject that I cover in more detail under the section Destiny, Freedom of Choice, and Invocation (prayers). To briefly introduce this topic, I have designed the chart below based on the teachings of many scholars. It should clarify the role prayers play in your life and the time lapse which may be instantaneous or some later time in your life or only ever rewarded on Judgment day. This is also a sensitive and difficult subject to explain because it relates not only to the relationship between destiny and prayers, but also freewill, all of which will later be covered in greater detail.

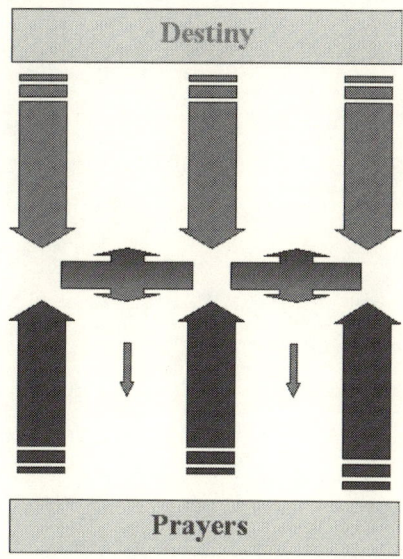

> Islamic Scholars agree that destined hardships and difficulties (and also good fortune) "descend" (approaches its destined time) and are met by raising invocations (prayers); they struggle until the Day of resurrection. If your prayers are weaker than this destined misfortune, then it will find its way to you but its impact may be reduced to various degrees; or good fortune may multiply as it interacts with your prayers. You will better understand this after reading the section on Destiny, Freewill, and Invocation (Prayers). I will also later provide you with a list of Hadiths and verses that are of relevance to this topic.

You will later read about the tie between destiny and freedom of choice as I risk plunging head first into the deep end of Islam to extract in simple terms what the reality is on this tough subject; but for now, here is one Hadith that is relevant to "asking" for what you want.

The Prophet (pbuh) said: "A servant's prayers (invocations) continue to be answered (by God) so far as he does not pray for a sin or a break of family ties (responsibilities towards family) and so long as he does not hurry it (become impatient)." It was said "O prophet of Allah (God)! What is hurry (impatience in supplication)?" He said, "That one says I have prayed and prayed and I was not answered. And at that he loses faith and abandons supplication."[14] So, yes, it is important to have faith and continue to pray.

I will later provide you with a list of Hadiths and verses from which you can extract the best times for prayers to be answered, and the most effective ways to ask for what you want.

---

14 Authentic hadith in Sahih Muslim number 2735

4. **Gratitude and the morning gratefulness routine.** The Law of Attraction gurus have now found out that being grateful supports the process of getting what you want (more of what you have been blessed with). Islam had stated this centuries ago. Surat Al-'Imran says:

"...Allah will reward the grateful",

Quran 3:144

and similarly...

"... we will reward the grateful",

Quran 3:145

Furthermore, the Prophet Mohammed (pbuh), in many of his teachings urges that we ask our Lord for all matters concerning this life and the afterlife.

Under "The Secret Summary" paragraph, you may have noticed that I have the words "morning gratefulness routine" in italics text. That is because in Islam, there ARE daily morning routine prayers that include being grateful for all that you have been blessed with. Keep in mind that as I am referring to "prayers," I do not mean the mandatory five prayers a day that most people know are key to the Muslim faith. I am simply referring to the act of wording your "wants" (forgiveness, heaven, wealth...) and praising God. Basically, this is the act of invocation. These daily morning prayer (invocation) routines give thanks for all blessings, give praise to the creator, and ask of his blessings (health, wealth, success....); the key difference here is that now, your feeling grateful is complete. You are **aware** and are **intentionally** being grateful to the proper source of what you are grateful for. You might have sensed the awkwardness and almost hypocritical aura one gives when being just "thankful." To whom is he or she being thankful? **Knowing what to be thankful for does not fulfill the need to know whom to be thankful to.**

5. It is you who is attracting all those "negative" events in your life. (What is negative in your life is your doing). Read the following:

   In Surat an-Nisa' we are told:

"What comes to you of good is from Allah, but what comes to you of evil, [O mankind], is from yourself [a result of your mistakes or sins]..."

Quran 4:79

And in Surat an-Nahl:

"And whatever you have of favor is from Allah. Then when adversity touches you, to Him you cry for help. Then when He removes the adversity from you, at once a party of you associates others with their Lord."

Quran 16:53–54

Also in Surat Ash-shura:

"And whatever strikes you (happens to you) of disaster (negative event)—it is for what your hands have earned, but He (Allah) pardons much."

Quran 42:30

So again, for different reasons than the ones presented in the video *The Secret*, I do agree with the point that you are the one attracting those negative events to your life, by the choices you have made or lack of when you should have. Again, always remember that to change your life, you must first change what is within yourself. You now know this ultimate law, and now you may begin to see how it works as I later give you the keys of how to use it.

Some of you may think that this is rather harsh or cruel, and may be quick to come up with counter arguments, supported by examples of poor hunger and disease-ridden children. "What have they done to deserve this?" I can hear some of you asking. Here, you should remember that these Ayat are not merely aimed at the individual, and here you should appreciate the collective social implications of their meaning. It is up to each individual in any society to be proactive against injustice. The Prophet—peace be upon him—said that each individual should actively oppose or seek to correct injustice; each to the level of influence they have been blessed with:

- a. By force (if you are in position to do so).
- b. By your words. (includes writing and other modern media)
- c. Condemning it secretly within your heart (This is generally for the weak and oppressed).[15]

By force refers to that group of people who are in position to do so in relation to the situation. For example, parents at home, the police in society and politicians in government. By words is the second category and it includes all those

---

15 From the authentic narration in Sunan Al-Nasa'i, number 5008.

who have no direct authority over the situation. This verbal condemnation of injustice does carry a lot of power because it will strengthen the community and it will ensure that those in power realize and notice the injustice. The third and weakest way is to condemn it secretly by heart and this is for those who may be under such oppressive regimes that they are not even allowed to speak up against injustice. By doing so, one can at least teach his heart to remain pure, and avoid contributing to the injustice. Furthermore, the unconscious signals communicated may have some positive behavior correcting effect on those whom are inflicting this injustice. Condemning injustice secretly within the heart is not simply for the weak and oppressed but is actually said to be for those with weak faith.

Keep in mind that within what you perceive as negative or positive, there are tests by which your reactions too will be judged. This is said in Surat al-Anbiya':

"Every soul will taste death, and we test you with evil and with good (good fortune and bad) as trial and to us you will be returned."

Quran 21:35

6. You are a miraculous being with the ability to use your mind, your heart (emotions), and your senses to seek all that you desire. The universe is on your side. It will "arrange" it for you. This concept is not too foreign to Islamic teachings but is worded differently and more accurately as follows:

"We have certainly created humans in the best of stature."

Quran 95:4

While swearing by his creation, the creator continues in Surat ash- Shams:

"And [by] the soul and He who proportioned it, and inspired it, [with discernment] its wickedness and its righteousness, He has succeeded who purifies it, and he has failed who instills it [with corruption]."

Quran 91:7–10

And in Surat Luqman we are asked:

"Do you not see that Allah has made subject{subservient} to you what-ever is in the heavens {the universe} and whatever is in the earth, and amply bestowed upon you his favors {both} apparent and unapparent? {But} of the people is he who disputes about Allah without knowledge or guidance or an enlightening book {from him}."

Quran 31:20

You have been created in the best of stature and you were also inspired with perception and judgment (discernment). We all have been blessed with the freedom of choice, the necessary senses, and a miraculous brain to support us in this process. Later, you will read how this freedom of choice interacts with your destiny.

7. That everything there is always was. That we are some sort of mini gods who can create things with our thoughts. That we can live however we want and we will never be judged.

Previously, you read how **scientists know for a fact that the universe did not always exist**. Clear evidence, Islamic and scientific, that **what was presented in the**

movie in a way insinuating that it's a fact was indeed FANTASY. It is wishful thinking and proven as false— the idea that everything there is always was. They claim that we are all energy and that energy always was and always will be, just like God. Setting the scene for the next "natural" and "logical" step that we will never Die . . . we will simply transform into something else on and on and on and no one will ever be judged, or held accountable for what they do. Man truly is a most self-deceiving creature. Surely, you see that this is further evidence that indeed as previously stated, **we make our decisions based on emotion and then use logic to justify our actions**. Most likely, emotions that encompass a great deal of fear (Fear held back by just as great an amount of denial). "There's a psychiatrist in Brazil named Norberto Keppe who suggests that the most common human mental illness is what he calls Theomania: the delusion that we human beings can be God" (Peck, 1993, p.192).

In his book, *Further along the Road Less Traveled*, M. Scott Peck (1993) says, "We all go around suffering from Theomania, the illusion that we can be the scriptwriter in the drama of our lives, and we become furious, depressed, or terrified when things don't go as we would have written the script or wanted them to go. In fact, many of us are never able to adjust to the reality that life is larger than something that is just our show" (p.193).

Peck also later mentions the first commandment "I am the lord thy God, and thou shalt not have any other gods before me" (p.224). This verse is part of the bible text which

I believe is among those parts that managed to remain as close to the original script as possible.

This reminds me of this verse from Surat Az Zukhruf:

"[But] they have attributed to Him {Allah} from his servants a portion*. Indeed man is clearly ungrateful."

Quran 43:15

I now see this statement was not just limited to those claiming that God has a son or daughters, as a child is part of his parents, but also to those claiming that we too are part of "that which we call God."

God also asks in the Quran if they have witnessed this creation. In Surat Yunus, The Most Merciful says in the Quran:

"And most of them follow not except assumption. Indeed, assumption avails not against the truth at all,..."

Quran 10:36

THE ULTIMATE LAW OF CHANGE

To change your condition, you must change what is within you.

This is The Ultimate Law of the human condition, whether as a society or an individual. Every single human development field has been trying in varying ways to do just that. Personal development and human potential fields, in the many methods they have come up with, are basically attempting to change what is within. Some focused on emotions, others on thoughts and some on beliefs, then they realized that they are all connected and that to achieve best results, none of these elements should be neglected in the process.

You may be thinking at this stage *Okay, so I must change what is within me, but what do I need to change and HOW*. First, you already know that you will be working with your thoughts, emotions, and beliefs; key to add at this point is that your intentions are also part of this change mixture. The next paragraph will clarify some of the details involved in the process of change.

Your past experiences set up your future. They are the reference points you use when making decisions. Even when you learn something new and intellectually understand it, it will not be sufficient on its own to change your behavior. This is part of the reason smokers who know and understand intellectually the dangers of smoking still continue to smoke. Christian H. Godefroy (2001), in his book titled *Mind Powers How to Use and Control Your Unlimited Potential*, explains under the subject of Psychocybernetics that "An intellectual understanding is not enough to guide your behavior in an effective way—you also need experience" (p.114). Experience is what your self-image is based upon. Why is self-image relevant? Godefroy continues to say that this is because your subconscious mind will always protect your self-image and "Trying to do things that run counter to our self-image will inevitably result in failure" (p.114). Now because experience requires so much time and the process of gaining it can sometimes be painful or dangerous, it pleases me to give you the good news that there IS a safer Shortcut: Your imagination! Your subconscious mind cannot tell the difference between real experience and what is imagined. I often use the well-known "lemon" example to prepare subjects (usually interested friends or family members) for hypnosis and it clearly proves this point. By simply vividly imagining a lemon (its color, its smell), slicing it in half, then biting it would make you salivate. Basically, as Godefroy

(2001) explains, "Our self-image is affected just as much by what we vividly imagine as by what we actually experience" (p.116). Confused? Allow me to clarify and at the same time give you the methods by which you can utilize your imagination to gain experience.

I will not presume to know or dictate upon you what you need to change, but having decided what you want or need to change, you will now learn methods that support how you can achieve those goals. These methods are designed to supplement good scheduling, not replace it.

THE METHODS

a. The Visualization Method

Experience is what self-image is based on and self-image is closely guarded by the unconscious mind, which explains why so many attempts for change result in failure. You must change this self-image if you are to secure any lasting change in your life. So experience is the best tool for change because it is what will alter the perhaps crippling self-image that you may have, especially with respect to the perceived problem you wish to resolve or goal you wish to achieve. The experience itself does not need to be real in order to utilize it for change. This is where the potential for hypnosis (or self-hypnosis) comes in as a great tool to ensure quality of these imagined experiences.

Hypnosis or self-hypnosis will give you greater control over the results of these experiences allowing greater success. Naturally, these experiences will incorporate thoughts, emotions, beliefs, and intentions; otherwise, how realistic can they be? Again, this can easily be accomplished with the proper use of hypnosis. This is what I mean by the "**visualization method**." The elements that make up this method are not new, nor is the suggestion to use hypnosis for change. Use it, making sure that you first actually know what you want to achieve. You may find it helpful to write it down in detail. Visualize yourself living the goals you will achieve. Reading over some of the hypnosis induction scripts and understanding them will deepen your ability to relax when applying this method. Then simply feel and absorb the experience of mentally living over and over the situation successfully and full of confidence. Place yourself there, behaving, thinking, and acting in the exact manner that you WILL.

b. Rehearsals

Another great method for gaining experience but under relative control is through the use of "**rehearsals**." It can be used concurrently with the previous method of visualization. You could use rehearsals by day and visualization by night, keeping in mind that visualization without hypnosis can and should be part of rehearsals.

Rehearsals are the method of choice for so many professional organizations in preparation for any important task or activity. Professional armies, like the British Army, who often are required to work under pressure to achieve extremely difficult objectives, rely heavily on rehearsals. Very often in these modern armies, individuals are required to develop and maintain high standards of skills: skills necessary to simultaneously maintain communications with other units (each with its own aims and main efforts), while also maintaining command and control. All this while remaining flexible enough to solve the waves of difficulties that arise with the never-ending situational changes that occur on the complex modern battlefield. Being a graduate of the Royal

Military Academy Sandhurst (RMAS),[16] I have witnessed firsthand the importance and effectiveness of rehearsals, whether on a physical level, mental, or a mix of the two.

How to use it? Let us say you are asked by the company you work for to give a presentation about a certain service the company provides to potential clients. You gather all the material together and prepare a great presentation. So far, it is only great on paper. On the day, a multitude of things can go wrong. However, by actually giving the presentation several times to an imaginary audience, you can resolve any problems before the actual event. Every attempt should be made to keep your rehearsals as realistic as possible; preferably, in the same location the event is to take place (or at least a similar one). So if possible, rehearse in the room or hall the event is to take place. Every detail, even speaking out loud to the empty chairs in front of you in the exact manner you wish to do so on the day is important. Keep track of timings or whatever restrictions that may be imposed upon you. You will gain the experience without the pressure of a live audience. By the time you do give the presentation, you will already have the backing of the confidence and security that comes with experience. On the day, you will feel as if you have been doing this all your life and it will be great.

Done properly, rehearsals WILL give you the experience you need to accomplish any task. Magicians, martial artists, and, as already mentioned, armies, all use rehearsals as a **vital** part of their training. Notice that all three fields deal with achieving difficult and sometimes seemingly impossible feats. Because of my background in all three of these fields, I can guarantee you that it would be close to impossible to

---

16 RMAS is the British Army's officer training academy believed by many to be the best military officer-commissioning course worldwide. For more information, visit the Academy's website at www.sandhurst.mod.uk/.

achieve any measurable amount of success in any one of them without rehearsals (practice).

Rehearsals do have one weakness and that is the element of time. The situation may be that you do not have enough time to conduct the number of rehearsals you would like in order to reach higher levels of confidence. Here I recommend that you try to fit one in using your imagination. Use the visualization method already discussed to complete at least one rehearsal. Try to let your imagination compensate for reality as much as possible. This may be slightly more difficult because a lack of time will also limit the visualization method to just imagination without the support of hypnosis. Yet, this can still be of great value and turn an average or poor performance to a very good one. I personally have rehearsed for speeches using the imagination part of the visualization method to prepare for them. By simply going to bed early and practicing using my mind only, I was able to perform flawlessly the next day. This of course requires that you actually know the material you will be speaking about. This can be achieved through repetition of rehearsals. This leads to the two key guidelines you should follow when using both visualization and rehearsals:

1. Realistic visualization: Try to visualize the event as realistically as possible.
2. Repetition: Repeating the process several times.

Both methods support change by providing the individual with reference points in the form of experience. This experience will alter his or her self-image and once that is done, your subconscious mind will now work for you, not against you, in maintaining this self-image. In other words, many people fail to change because of a subconscious resistance which is basically the mind protecting its self-image. What you have done now is alter this self-image which is built on reference points by providing new reference points through experience, because experience builds strong reference points. Furthermore, the unconscious mind can be influenced by vividly imagined experiences as much as the real experience. We are utilizing this shortcut to maximize experience in as short a time as possible and under much more controllable circumstances.

The use of visualization has of late gained a lot of popularity within the sports community. It is being used to enhance performance with fast and measurable results. In an article titled "Visualization" which deals with this type of use, it is explained that, "Research has been done showing that when someone visualizes something, the exact same neurons in the brain are fired as if the person was actually doing the activity! Those neural connections are strengthened simply by thinking of the activity!" (www.golfnosis.com, 2008).

Sports psychologist Dr. Jack Singer (2008) explains that practitioners in his field are now teaching self-hypnosis to athletes helping them with skills such as intensity, focus, consistency, concentration, anxiety, and anger control. Singer also says that: "While under hypnosis, my athlete is not only visualizing success in his next game, but he is planting optimistic seeds in the beautiful garden of his subconscious mind that are each related to specific moves and strategies that are designed to work against a specific opponent, whom he can visualize defeating" (www. howtousesportspsychology.com).

Do not let all this shift your focus to short-term performance success in some small feat you wish to excel in, such as, perhaps, publicly speaking at some venue. While visualization and rehearsals will greatly enhance your performance in such tasks, do remember the greater potential here: a way to purposefully alter your self-image in a controlled environment! The importance of this, if not already self-evident, should become clear as you read the sections below, just past the next few paragraphs which briefly examine the role of prayers.

What remains now to be added under methods is Invocation. Praying for what you want will give you the faith you need to persevere and will keep you focused on what it is you want, both of which are vital for accomplishing your goals. Keep in mind that your prayers are being answered by The Creator, not some good luck charm hung around your neck. Human sciences have matured a great deal lately, but unfortunately in doing so have begun to disregard the important role of prayers and faith. This is partly because as science matured, it began to notice faults in religions that underwent human interference and alteration of their original form. This in time led to a situation now where scientists, even those "religious" ones, are often afraid of involving any religious influence in their works. This is out of an unfortunate, yet realistic fear that they will be compartmented and then removed from the scientific community like they were some sort of computer virus. This is because their findings may pose a threat to the "system."

On the one hand is the visualization method which is geared more towards personal and character changes as well as healing, motivation, and other similar aspects of life. On the other hand are rehearsals which are more for developing your practical, physical, and other performance skills. Invocation will supplement both methods and it will strengthen your spirit which will boost and charge up both your mind and body. You will learn more about invocation soon, along with other Islamic insight on change and success.

c. The Time Factor

It is appropriate here to add that there is a time factor in this equation as well. This becomes of much greater importance if your goal is to change a behavioral problem of yours. Your choices, especially when followed by action, create behavioral patterns. The secret to long-term success for the decisions you make is repetition and repetition takes time. Repetition will strengthen this new "path" you have selected and its corresponding neuro- connections in your brain.

To better understand these neuro-connections, imagine a dense forest. If you were to force yourself to walk from one end of the forest to the next, the path you take will be difficult and probably disappear within a few days. Now imagine that you take this same path every day for forty days. The second or third time you take the same path may be difficult to follow and still slow going territory with the possibility of getting lost. After thirty or more times, the path will have become well defined and clear. It would be difficult to get lost on the way. Even if you leave it for a few days, it would take much longer for the forest to obscure it. Likewise are the behavioral patterns within you. The more times you repeat any behavior, the more likely it is that you will do so in the future and again all this requires time.

DECISIONS (CHANGE AND CHOICES)

While the methods involved in long-term change and developing new habits and skills are relatively time consuming, the actual change is not. Change is something that happens in a moment. Change is the moment you make a choice, **a decision towards a goal, not a decision away from a fault**. This is because deciding to stop or remove something from your life creates a void that if you do not purposefully fill, may remain an empty home readily furnished to host that which you had attempted to get rid of. This is one reason that makes it easy for old habits to return. You must fill this space in order to prevent reemergence of what you decided to get rid of. Keep in mind that by simply adding a new positive behavior to your life you should also be automatically replacing a negative behavior. Now you are in a great position to reinforce this behavior because instead of focusing on what you do not want by trying to combat a behavior, you are now focusing on what you do want by simply doing it. This way, you are automatically replacing an "occupant" behavior, not just removing one. For example, you may want to stop watching television for six hours a day because you know you need more exercise and it is wasting your time. Do not try to stop watching television, simply start going to the gym and scheduling your exercise time to replace your normal television watching hours. In fact, most gyms now have screens attached to most of the running/ walking machines and bikes. Remember that by simply doing anything; you increase the likelihood of redoing so at a later date.

Decision points (choices) are what guide your destiny. Remember this when reading the section on Destiny, Freewill, and Invocation. With this new emphasis on choices, it is only appropriate that I provide you with a mental guard to ensure that you understand how others are trying to manipulate your freedom of choice. The decisions you make WILL shape your destiny and I think that it's only fair that you hold that power in your own hands (by shaping destiny, I mean that this occurs within destiny' preset limits which will be explained later on). You already understand the role emotions play in your decision- making cycle and now you will discover how words can also be used for that purpose.

THE POWER OF WORDS OVER DECISIONS

Having read this far, you are ready to appreciate the power of words over decisions, which is related to "the power of suggestion." This section is partly based on an article titled "When Words Decide" by Barry Schwartz (2007) because I thought that it clearly presented the topic. To further develop your sense of awareness to the environment you live in and to make better personal choices, you need to understand the role words play in "your" decision making. Schwartz (2007) explains, "The phrasing of questions or choices can have a profound, and often counterintuitive, effect on the way people make decisions" (p.38). This is due to the alteration of one's perception of "loss-versus-gain." When making choices, people are basically evaluating the loss versus gain based upon what they perceive as being lost or gained.

In *The Prospect Theory*, "Kahneman and Tcersky deciphered the relation between the objective and the subjective as it relates to losses and gains" (Schwartz, 2007, p. 39).

On deciding between two choices, Schwartz (2007) explained that while people's satisfaction does increase when the outcome increases favorably, this satisfaction "does not increase in linear fashion in relation to the gain," (p. 39), so double the positive outcome is not double the satisfaction. In fact, Schwartz further adds, "A person's subjective state improves at an increasingly slower rate until an objective improvement in situation hardly changes a person's satisfaction at all—something economists call "diminishing marginal utility...." When it comes to negative occurrences such as deaths, changes in a person's emotional state similarly diminish as the situation worsens rather than continuing to worsen at a rate proportional to the circumstances" (p.39).

This only sounds complicated but it's not. Basically, diminishing marginal utility is a system in which the same input continues to output less and less until that same input results in almost no output. How this is related to decision making will soon become apparent when you see how marketers and politicians are using this information to manipulate your choices and the decisions you make.

Furthermore, with respect to decision-making factors, you should realize that as Schwartz put it, "people are risk averse when contemplating gains," (p.39) but they are more likely to take risks when contemplating losses. This means that you are more likely to enter risky ventures when worried about what you may lose than you are if simply contemplating what you may gain. "Whether people are attending to gains or losses depends on how the options are framed" (p.39).

Knowing this, you may now begin to see how those in power are utilizing this knowledge when presenting their cases by carefully wording the way they present options for consumption by the masses.

The wording of sentences in speeches or questions is vital to manipulating how people perceive a situation. They allow a person to set the defaults and context which greatly affects perception. The **power** of **default**[17] and **context**[18] are subtopics of the above paragraph and they too will further open your eyes and fine tune your hearing to the daily force-feeding your mind goes through by a powerful and determined media. There are many examples to draw from in order to demonstrate the power of the **default** choice. I could also call it the choices you never made, because by nature, a default choice is not something you actively must decide. By simply remaining silent or not deciding, the decision is made for you.

The following example provided by Schwartz (2007) will clarify what this means: "Decision scientists Eric J. Johnson of Columbia University and Daniel Goldstein, now at London Business School,

---

17 By default, I mean the outcome which will automatically result, due to the absence of a decision or action.
18 By context, I am referring to the scene or environment and/or words used to set a situation and its perceived constraints and boundaries.

reported in 2003, more than ninety percent of the people in many European countries are organ donors, whereas only about twenty-five percent of Americans are" (p.40). It is explained that to be an organ donor in the U.S. you had to sign up for it while in those European countries it was the *default choice*, meaning you had to sign up not to be one!

Likewise, I have noticed lately that many restaurants are following this principle by adding "tipping" (service charge) automatically to the bill. Often, you do have the right to revoke it, but how many people will?

People are often too distracted or too lazy to be proactive and seem to view the default choice as the safe bet. I believe that this is also due to the assumption that someone better informed about the topic already made the decision that this is the best choice. I also believe that it implies most people have chosen, or would choose, this option, allowing a form of indirect peer pressure to be involved.

According to Schwartz's article (2007), a third major influence on the choices we make is context (p.41). Basically, context dictates what you compare an option to. Instead of comparing your choice to something that may seem better, you are presented the choice "they" want you to take while comparing it to a much worse option. Suddenly, that price or personal sacrifice you would normally avoid does not seem so terrible. Just think of how many "personal freedom reduction laws" were passed in the West by framing them within a terrorism-associated context. Buying this book means that you are interested in gaining more control over your life and therefore you must deepen your understanding of how others may be making your decisions for you. It is vital if you want to achieve "your" goals that "you" make the decisions towards those goals. Believe me, if you don't run your own life, there are many who are interested in running it for you (often for their own interests). Here are two examples that clearly highlight how words affect your decisions from the previous source. They should completely clarify how this knowledge is used to influence your choices.

The first shows that "the language of choice not only affects what we choose but also—eerily—our sensory experiences of that choice.... People will choose a hamburger that is 75 percent lean over one that is 25 percent fats, but when they actually taste the two hamburgers (which are, of course, two versions of the same hamburger), the 75 percent lean burger actually tastes better. So although it may seem irrational to prefer one hamburger over another physically identical one, if the burger that is called "75 percent lean" tastes better than the one dubbed "25 percent fat," perhaps it makes sense to prefer that one after all" (Schwartz, 2007, p.42).

This second example also from the previous source highlights how policy makers and those in power can use this knowledge to manipulate you. Which is not necessarily always a bad thing, but in this case, you be the judge.

"When Bush and his allies in Washington launched their campaign against the estate tax, they relabeled it the 'death tax.' Think of what this label does. Who pays the death tax? The dead person does. As if dying were not bad enough, the government reaches into the grave to extract its pound of silver. Worse yet, the dead person has already paid taxes on that money, when it was originally earned. Now suppose that instead of calling it a 'death tax,' we called it an 'inheritance tax.' Who pays the inheritance tax? The living do—and, unlike the dead, they have never paid taxes on these assets before. The same tax seems much more attractive and fair under that label," (p.43).

In other words, if the U.S. had announced that it will now tax people on what they inherit, people would have strongly objected to it; but because instead of calling it inheritance tax they called it death tax, people never objected to it. The context made it seem that this is something that will affect them after they die rather than while alive, and they completely forgot that something is being taken away from them.

PRIMING

By now, we are prepared for the introduction of the concept of **priming**, and its relevance to context. Together, they manipulate modern man via mass media to such an extent that modern thinker Malcolm Gladwell (2005) says, "What we think of as free will is largely an illusion"; that "the way we think and act—and how well we think and act on a spur of the moment—are a lot more susceptible to outside influence than we realize" (p.58). I believe that the best way to grasp the idea of priming is through an example from Gladwell's book, *Blink* (2005). He describes a test (a priming experiment) devised by the psychologist John Bargh. The experiment was conducted at New York University by Bargh, Mark Chen, and Lara Burrows:

They used a group of undergraduates as subjects and gave everyone in the group one of two scrambled—sentence tests. The first was sprinkled with words like "aggressively," "bold," "rude," "bother," "disturb," "intrude," and "infringe." The second was sprinkled with words like "respect," "considerate," "appreciate," "patiently," "yield," "polite," and "courteous." In neither case were there so many similar words that the students picked up on what was going on. (Once you become conscious of being primed, of course, the priming doesn't work.) After doing the test—which takes only about five minutes—the students were instructed to walk down the hall and talk to the person running the experiment in order to get their next assignment.

Whenever a student arrived at the office, however, Bargh made sure that the experimenter was busy, locked in conversation with someone else—a confederate who was standing in the hallway, blocking the doorway to the experimenter's office. Bargh wanted to learn whether the people who were primed with polite words would take longer to interrupt the conversation between the experimenter and the confederate than those primed with the rude words. He knew enough about the strange power of unconscious influence to feel that it would make a difference, but he thought the effect would be slight (p.54).

The circumstances restricted the total waiting time for each subject to not exceed 10 minutes. So what were the results?

The people primed to be rude eventually interrupted—on average after about five minutes. But of the people primed to be polite, the overwhelming majority—82 percent—never interrupted at all. (Gladwell, 2005, p.55)

This experiment by Bargh and his partners clearly highlights the inner force of words over perception and eventually the decisions we make. So how can you use this to your advantage in guiding change within your life? Previously under methods for change, I spoke of visualization and rehearsals along with invocation. You can now add to that an experiment I am sure will greatly change your life. Choose one negative word that is quite popular within your daily vocabulary then remove and replace it with a positive, more optimistic word. Now choose any negative basic belief you may have, regardless of whether it's true or not, and reword it using positive words. You don't need to change the meaning of your belief, just the way it is presented. For example, "I'm so cruel" can be changed to "I'm not very kind." This simple tactic is so powerful especially on the long run. It is one more way to influence your self-image consciously. What would happen in your life if you applied this to five negative words and five beliefs you have about yourself? How about ten? What if you adopt this one strategy and make it a general rule or value within your life? So far, much of what we discussed under The Power of Words over Decisions and even under much of what was covered previously is related to context. Context that surely many lawyers' and judges know is key to the decisions and judgments made every day in courts around the world. This is historically not a new issue. Over fourteen centuries ago, the Prophet Mohammed (pbuh) spoke of how words (altering context and therefore perception) can affect judgment. In this case not personal but legal. An example of this is when by teaching his followers about justice, he said:

"You come to me (seeking judgment) and I am but human, and some of you may better 'word' your case (is more clever with words, more eloquente and more convincing) and I give my judgment in his favor according to what I hear. Beware! If ever I give (by error) somebody something of his brother's right then he should not take it as I have only, given him a piece of Fire."."[19] As a note this above narration not only highlights the power of words to prime people or set the context in favor of outcomes. More critically it was highlighting that the ability to use the right words and eloquently paint with them the context should not be used against those who cannot in order to take what is rightfully theirs. Such verbal agility can be used for the wrong reasons. Even if a court of law judges in your favor due to your superior abilities in language (and your opponent's inability to properly express his case) then it is still unjust for you to take other people's rights even if the legal court judged in your favor.

A vital difference between the ultimate law of change and much of what was presented in the Law of Attraction is the presence of the mother of all sins, **pride**. In man's quest to tighten his grip upon this world through science and other methods, he has become more proud

---

[19] The authentic narration from Sahih Al-Bukhari, hadith number 6967, also narrated by several others.

of his achievements. So proud that he attempts to avoid all that may suggest that in fact all he has done was to provide the reasons, when it was a greater power other than him/her that has made all this possible in the first place. We forget that it was a greater power that set the laws and that all we can ever do is discover them. Some choose to marvel at the magnificence of what The Creator has created and others seem to be blinded by pride, as if what they have discovered or developed was their own creation. Many of us seem to have forgotten that all we can ever achieve is governed and limited by laws that we have had no say or choice in their creation.

The social arts of choice manipulation continue to be developed and refined primarily fueled by those who are not the least bit concerned about your freewill or wellbeing. By now, you are aware of how much choice manipulation is done at an unconscious level. Remembering this targeting of the unconscious is very important for you to now appreciate the significance of what I am about to tell you next. **Much of the choices you think you are consciously making have in fact already been *decided* by "you" unconsciously.**

Nicole Branan (2008), in Scientific American Mind magazine wrote that:

A team led by John-Dylan Haynes of the Bernstein Center for Computational Neuroscience Berlin scanned the brains of volunteers who held a button in each hand and were told to push one of the buttons whenever they wanted to. The scientists could tell from the scans which hand participants were going to use as early as ten seconds before the volunteers were aware that they made up their mind.

Previous research has shown motor-related brain activity preceding conscious intent by a fraction of a second, but this study is the first to show unconscious predictive activity in a region associated with decision making—the prefrontal cortex (p.8).

The above article further explains that "the results support the notion that unconscious brain activity comes first and conscious experience follows as a result" (p.8).

Of relevance to note here is the article's reference to the relationship between the prefrontal cortex and decision-making. In fact, the front part of your head (frontal lobe) is not only responsible for decision making, but also motivation planning, reasoning, parts of speech, and cost-benefit analysis among other things. This new discovery by modern science conforms to what the Quran stated fourteen centuries ago. When discussing lying and sinful actions, the Quran specifically and purposefully ties between those actions to that part of the head in which the Prefrontal Cortex is. This as usual is stated in a casual, and matter of fact manner which reads as follows:

> *"No! if he does not desist, we will surely drag him by the Naseyah, a lying sinning Naseyah."*
>
> Quran 96:15–16

Naseyah in Arabic literally refers to the front of the head just behind the forehead and between the temples. This is exactly where you find that part of the brain now scientifically referred to as the prefrontal cortex!

In fact, it is almost ironic to read some of the titles of recent articles describing the latest scientific discoveries with respect to the prefrontal cortex. Some of them are:

"Liar, Liar, Your Prefrontal Cortex Is On Fire" Article by Kate Melville.[20]

---

[20] http://www.scienceagogo.com/news/20050904005107data trunc sys.shtml (retrieved 13/12/2016)

Here the connection between lying and the prefrontal cortex (the "Naseyah" area) is clearly referred to in the title itself.

> "Moral Decision-Making and the Ventromedial Prefrontal Cortex" article by Johan in Emotion, Neuroscience, Social Neuroscience.[21]

Here, too, the connection is made clear between the prefrontal cortex and the making of immoral or moral decisions.

You realize now that change is a decision. It only takes a few moments to change, not years. The effects of change and results may take longer to manifest. Success lies in following up on those decisions with action. First **decide**, then **plan**, and finally you must **take action**. This can clearly be concluded by studying some of the Hadith that point to this.

Having searched a number of books that narrate Hadith, I have found, as common sense would assert, knowledge should always come before action. Knowledge of course is a vital part of the decision-making and planning process. Therefore, decisions should ideally come after the accumulation of enough knowledge, followed by the actions of planning, then implementation.

Some thinkers place planning prior to deciding but the fact is that true planning can only be accomplished after a decision is made. You need to be clear about what you are planning for. **Good decisions are not the result of planning; they are the result of knowledge and clear values.** This is one more reason why Islam places so much emphasis on the pursuit of knowledge (education). Planning comes later and serves the practical aspects of how to achieve the objectives of decisions, not what they are. Here I am referring to long-term objectives,

---

21 https://phineasgage.wordpress.com/2007/03/23/moral-decision-making-and-the-ventromedial-prefrontal-cortex/ (retrieved 13/12/2016.)

because short-term objectives often can be the result of planning as stepping stones towards a goal or long-term objective.

While planning is very important, it remains secondary and has a somewhat inferior role. This secondary role will surely be appreciated by military officers and planners because they know that no plan survives the first "step" ("first shot" or "first contact"). Through experience, they know that once plans are set in motion, they immediately succumb to situational changes due to unforeseen circumstances. Having trained as a military officer, I can assure you that flexibility is one of the most important characteristics of a realistic plan. A clear objective or aim and intent are far more important than a "perfect" plan. The focus should remain on "what" you want while keeping the "how" part subservient to flexibility and creativity.

I know this to be true through experience. It seems that determination and perseverance play a more important role in reaching goals. The nature of life is such that change remains to be the only constant. Therefore, situational changes will always render strict plans useless. The best plans are those that are most flexible, with clear objectives; objectives based on knowledge and values. This is important because the perseverance or commitment towards a goal can only be maintained if in return those goals are based on personal values (values being the result of the belief framework in an individual).

GRATEFULNESS AND INVOCATION

GRATEFULNESS

I found it to be very arrogant to just be grateful, avoiding the question "To whom am I grateful to?" **Knowing what to be thankful for**

does not substitute the need for knowing whom to be thankful to. Similarly, when asking for what you want, it is not enough to just know what you want. You might as well choose a pen or a rock and ask it for what you want. The case here is not simply that of ignorance, it is surely one of arrogance, if not both.

Sincere gratitude requires clear intent and humbleness directed towards whom you perceive as the cause of the effect you are grateful for. Do take great care not to confuse The Creator with his creations. I believe that Surat Fatir says it best:

> *"Say, "Have you considered your 'partners' whom you invoke besides Allah? Show me what they have created from the earth, or have they partnership {with Him} in the heavens? {Or} have we given them a book so they are (standing) on evidence therefrom? (No), rather the wrongdoers do not promise each other except delusion (pride).""*
>
> Quran 35:40

Of relevance also is the following from Surah At-Tur:

> *"Or have they a deity other than Allah? Exalted is Allah above whatever they associate with him."*
>
> Quran 52:43

Within this book are several Ayat prompting gratitude to the Most Merciful, but who else should we be grateful and give thanks to? In other words, if you are to believe that all you have of wealth (health, money, family, friends, etc.) is from The Creator, then should you also thank people who are only tools through which God has blessed you? the answer is yes. The Prophet (pbuh) teaches us in the following Hadith and said:

"Whoever is not thankful (grateful) to people, is not grateful to God."[22]

INVOCATION

Previously, you read about the methods of visualization and rehearsals. Now you are prepared to supplement them with invocation. While the previous two methods may not require faith, invocation, on the other hand, is greatly dependent on belief. The following Hadith best explains the three outcomes possible for invocation and what some of the conditions are:

"Any Muslim who invokes God will be given by God one of three: either it will be answered (as in immediately or within his lifetime), or it will be kept for his benefit on the day of judgment, or it will be used to deter from him a harm of equal value as long as he does not ask for a sin or break of family ties and responsibilities"[23]

I have used this with a very high rate of success (as in earthly manifestation) and I here bear witness to the countless blessings of Allah. To truly utilize this form of method for success and getting what you want, read the list of Hadith and Ayat provided under the Relevant Quran and Hadith section to best magnify your rate of success. This list is a selection of Hadith from which you can extract important information to achieve successful invocation. Remember that invocation without effort will rarely produce results. Islam teaches that you need to provide the "reasons through actively working towards your goals. Here lies a great test of pride versus gratefulness, because without true faith, people who achieve their goals may become intoxicated with the

---

[22] The authentic narration from Jami' Al-Tirmithi, hadith number 1954. Also mentioned by other narrators.
[23] From the authentic narration narrated in Misnad Ahmed, hadith number 11149. Also narrated by many others.

sense of accomplishment and believe that it was their skills, efforts, or cleverness and knowledge that gained them this fortune. They forget who blessed them with this knowledge and that even with this knowledge a greater power is the true source of all that exists and manifests. To this the Quran in Surat Az- Zumar states:

"And when adversity touches man, he calls upon Us; then when We bestow on him a favor from Us, he says, "I have only been given it because of [my] Knowledge." Rather, it is a trial, but most of them do not know" (Quran 39:49).

DESTINY, FREEWILL, AND INVOCATION (PRAYERS)

In Islam, belief in destiny is a must if one is to be a true believer. A popular question is, "Well, if The Most Merciful already knows, and it has been written where we end up in life and afterlife, what are we working for?" This question mistakenly mixes between two separate issues. The first is that all of destiny has been written already and the second is that Allah (God) as The Creator has, as part of being The All-knowing, the characteristic of knowing everything that ever was, is, or will be. This second part is a higher form of knowledge that we must simply believe in on faith for we are not mentally capable of comprehending its details. The first part is what we are interested in. It is that "part" of destiny which we can "connect" with because man was created with both destiny *and* freedom of choice.

The above may seem complicated at a first glance. All I am saying really is that destiny can be split into two belief concepts that support each other. The first is that all destinies past and future have been written and nothing you do will change or alter what God has destined for you. The second is that within this destiny many things are written in a manner that allows freewill to dictate much of the events.

This second part of the belief in destiny was set in such fashion very similar to what you may relate to as cause and effect. It is written, for example, that if "X" son of "Y" cares for his mother and father when they can no longer care for themselves, then he will live the full ninety-five years of age destined for him; if, however, he "willingly" chooses to neglect them (especially in old age when they need much care and kindness), then "X" is to live only the eighty years of age also destined for him. For example, while one's time of death is totally part of the unknown and IS destined as an exact time, we are told in Surat Fatir that:

> "... and no aged person is granted [additional] life nor is his lifespan lessened but that it is in a register. Indeed, that for Allah is easy."
>
> Quran 35:11

Basically, while destiny has been written in a manner that makes it interact and react with "freewill" choices (The level of destiny we influence by the choices we make); God knows his creation and being all knowing, He has knowledge of every detail of his creation. Keeping in mind that "time" is a creation, realize that The Creator knows all things past, present, and future simultaneously. This level of destiny is beyond our comprehension.

Think about a computer game. As the player, you are restricted to the contents the programmer(s) has built into the game. Now think of those really complicated computer games that allow you to develop the character, meet other characters, develop relationships, and fight your way through a multitude of interconnected levels. Several of your friends may play the same game losing or winning in a multitude of ways. Now, remember that the best team of programmers, no matter how proud of their newly designed program, cannot compare to the creation of this universe.

The belief in destiny is inseparable from Islam. It is only in attempting to further clarify this topic that I have destiny divided into two levels:

1. That Allah is all-knowing and as such, in all His wisdom, holds this knowledge of the unknown to himself (The time of the day of resurrection, the time of your death, who will enter heaven or hell, etc.). This is for Muslims to believe in on faith and not dwell on.

2. Destiny was written in a manner that interacts with your freewill, and that you will be judged on the choices YOU make. The fact that your creator already knows what choices you will make is part of the higher level of destiny explained above. Here is where you focus your efforts. Here is where your free will can struggle for a better life in this lifetime and after resurrection. Using the programmer analogy, think of it as a matrix of if/else statements (if X does Y, then X gets T, else X gets Z).

Realize that believing in 'A' does not contradict your belief in 'B.' A simple example is:

A teacher knowing his students may accurately predict who will pass and who will fail, yet the students were freely able to choose whether to study or not; and to Allah is the highest form of this. Would the teacher fail or pass the students before the outcome of their choices? Is it the teacher who has failed them or have they failed themselves? The teacher, having provided them with the guidance they need, gave them a book to study from; would it not be unjust to those who answered correctly that those who never studied get the same grade?

The Prophet's companions who learned Islam directly from the Messenger himself (PBUH) understood this really well. One of the greatest companions of the Prophet (PBUH) and the second Caliph of Islam said something that clearly highlights this understanding.

As narrated in the authentic hadith, Abdullah bin Abbas said:

`Umar bin Al-Khattab [when he became Caliph] departed for Sham (the Levant region which today includes Syria, Palestine, and parts or Jordan) and when he reached Sargh (an area on the way just before or part of the outskirts of the Levant), the commanders of the (Muslim) army [in that region], Abu 'Ubaida bin Al-Jarrah and his companions met him and told him that an epidemic had broken out in Sham. `Umar said, "Call for me the early emigrants." [those who had migrated from Mecca to Medina with the prophet (pbuh)] So `Umar called them, consulted them and informed them that an epidemic had broken out in Sham. Those people differed in their opinions. Some of them said, "We have come out for a purpose and we do not think that it is proper to give it up," while others said (to `Umar), "You have along with you other people and the companions of Allah's Messenger (pbuh) so we do not advise that we take them to this epidemic." `Umar said to them, "Leave me now." Then he said, "Call the Ansar for me." I called them and he consulted them and they followed the way of the emigrants and differed as they did. He then said to them, Leave me now," and added, "Call for me the old people of Quraish who emigrated in the year of the Conquest of Mecca." I called them and they gave a unanimous opinion saying, "We advise that you should return with the people and do not take them to that (place) of epidemic." So `Umar made an announcement, "I will ride back to Medina in the morning, so you should do the same." Abu 'Ubaida bin Al-Jarrah [one of the aforementioned leaders who came to great Umar] said (to `Umar), "Are you running away from what Allah had destined (ordained)?" `Umar said, "Would that someone else had said such a thing, O Abu 'Ubaida! Yes, we are running from God's destiny towards God's destiny (or from what God had ordained to what God has ordained). Don't you agree that if you had camels that went down a valley having two places, one green and the other dry, you would graze them on the green one only if God had ordained that, and you would graze them on the dry one only if God had ordained that?" At that time `Abdulrahman bin `Auf, who had been absent because of some job, came and said, "I have some knowledge about this. I have heard God's Messenger (pbuh) saying, 'If you hear about it (an outbreak of plague) in a land, do not go to it; but if plague breaks out in a country where you are staying, do not run away from it.'" `Umar thanked and praised God then returned to Medina.[24]

Among the many lessons in this narration including the concept of plague containment, is the perfectly phrased understanding of destiny as we have previously described. By saying that one flees <u>from</u> God's destiny <u>to</u> God's destiny then giving the example of freedom of choice to where one grazes his herd animals, the wise Umar (RA) showed deep understanding of this concept. Just as in our previous metaphor the gamer was using his free-will but only within the limits the programmer had placed in the game, people too use their free-will to maneuver within destiny. The choices they make are critical. A strong emphasis in this book was placed on you reclaiming this freedom of choice from

---

[24] From the authentic narration in Sahih Albukhari, hadith number 5729. Also narrated by others.

the increasingly sophisticated tools used today by those who wish to control it.[25]

BEFORE WE CONCLUDE

The human body and mind is a spiritual creation. It thrives and functions most effectively when it is motivated by belief and faith. Faith and belief are often the source of motivation and perseverance that are vital in driving the individual and society to achieve whatever goals they may set forth. Throughout time, humanity has ridden the waves of the up and down fluctuation of this belief and faith system. (As humans, our faith wavers up and down; therefore, it is virtually impossible to maintain peak performance faith.) We are not angels; we have been created and preprogrammed to sin through a key element of humanity which is Forgetfulness. In fact, the Arabic word for human (Insan) has its roots in the word forgetful (Nisyan).

Throughout history, one can observe that change in all societies, whether it's the rise of a kingdom, the fall of an empire, or the birth of a nation. Part of the reason has always been a shift in people's beliefs. Likewise is the case on the level of a single individual.

Any individual seeking to truly reach his/her goals and dreams needs to have faith in something. The belief system an individual has is what will truly drives him or her forward because we are spiritual beings. Now it is your prerogative to choose what this will be.

---

[25] For more details on the "code" of destiny, when it was written and how it effects behavior even at the Quantum physics level please look forward to my work, currently subtitled, from Quantum physics to the flood. God willing when it is published it will cover such topics as creation, destiny, Quantum physics, the holographic universe, the big bang, the origin of matter, the 6 "days," DNA and genetics all in light of Islam and modern science.

However, it is highly beneficial if what you believe in is not simply part of creation, but in fact is The Creator.

You can make up or adopt principles and guidelines of your own to varying degrees of effectiveness, or use what was divinely designed for you. Humanity actually has been provided with several instruction manuals, but they were tampered with and changed and in fact some were only meant to be temporarily in effect for specific peoples. Finally we received the complete A-Z manual on all of life for humanity to be applicable to all of time untill the day of resurrection and to be protected and unchanged. It is the final message and it started with and continues to urge us to seek knowledge.

The Quran is intended for the final stage of humanity, to be a guide along with the prophet's teachings in a time of technology and science. Keeping in mind the unfortunate high rate of illiteracy and poor education within many Islamic societies, it is no mystery how politically motivated extremist groups are able to manipulate the feeble minded and ignorant by perverting and twisting religious ideals to better suit their wicked and un-Islamic objectives or methods.

After all, for nearly a thousand years people outside Islam were backward and in the dark. For example, while Europe was living in the dark ages, the Islamic world was the most advanced civilization both scientifically and socially.

Jews and other religiously discriminated groups fled to Muslim territory where freedom of worship was protected by Islamic law. Outside the Islamic world, women were treated terribly and were objects to be owned, often with no rights at all. In Europe, America, and other backward societies at the time, even men from different races were treated as inferior beings, if even human at all. Slavery was rampant and a thriving business, even in the Arab world.

Islam led the world in what still are international issues. Hundreds of years before racism was "legally" abolished, Islam had united all people as brothers and sisters and imbedded this on a personal belief system level (It was "what is within," not just political correctness). It teaches that the best of men/women are those most righteous and this can only be judged by The Creator Himself.

You now will read one of hundreds of Hadith that deal with the now hot topic of human rights. It will help illustrate Islam's view on slavery among other issues, and it goes as follows:

> The Messenger of Allah (pbuh) said that Allah the Almighty said:
>
> "There are three (types of people) whose adversary (against who) I shall be on the Day of Resurrection: a man who has given his word by Me and has broken it (gives a covenant and then proved himself treacherous); a man who has sold a free man (into slavery) and has consumed the price; and a man who has hired a workman, has exacted his due in full from him, but has not given him his wage."[26]

No matter how much the media tries to twist and misrepresent the truth, any educated women's rights activist will be quick to recognize that the Prophet Mohammed (pbuh) is in fact the first true liberator of women. He liberated women in the true essence of the word, not what some poor girl is tricked into thinking liberation is by man-driven industries that sell and use women as objects. Islam came at a time when in most of the world, women were seen as property and they lost ownership of any wealth to their husband upon marriage. Islam

---

26 From the authentic narration in Sahih Al-Bukhari, hadith number 2227. Also narrated by others.

came to give and protect women's rights to inheritance, ownership of private possessions and property, along with all other true freedoms and rights. It placed women at such a high status and this is reflected in many of the Prophet's teachings. We will state one that deals specifically with mothers as an example:

Perhaps the most well-known Hadith regarding this topic is about a man who asked the Prophet Mohammed (pbuh) "O Messenger of Allah! Who among all mankind warrants the best of my companionship, kindness, and care? He replied, "Your mother." The man asked, "Then who else?" The Prophet replied, "Your mother." The man asked (a third time), "Then who else?" The Prophet replied, "Your mother." The man asked a fourth time, "Then who else?" The Prophet replied, "Then your father."[27]

No one was above the law; even the Caliph (Ruler) or kings appeared before a judge as ordinary men in Islamic courts. In fact the great Caliph Ali (RA) himself once went to court because a Christian man had taken his chest plate armor. Despite being the Caliph and the husband of the Prophet's daughter and unquestionably an honest man with the highest degree of credibility the court ruled in favor of the Christian man. This was because Ali was unable to provide a witness beyond his son who also was rejected despite his unquestionable integrity and being the grandson of the Prophet (pbuh). The rejection was because a son cannot be an unbiased witness in favor of his father. Highly impressed by this the Jewish man embraced Islam and wanted

---

27 From the authentic narration in Sahih Al-Bukhari, hadith number 5971. Also narrated by many others.

to give back the chest armor but now Ali (RA) told him to keep it as a gift.[28]

Basically, Muslims led the world scientifically, morally, and socially... UNTIL many of them changed what is within themselves that in turn changed their condition. This again is another example of the law of change at work at the level of an entire society. When Muslims abandoned their unity and the requirement to seek knowledge and many other things their condition changed. After leading globally in many fields such as medical sciences, technology, engineering, mathematics, and astronomy this clearly is no longer the case.

Likewise was the case in Europe. One could argue about the causes and start of historical events such as the treaty of Westphalia in 1648 that ended the thirty years of war between the Catholics and Protestants and how it introduced respect for the rules of diplomacy; or can debate the significances of the Congress of Vienna in 1815 and other events that played a role in setting the grounds and planting the seeds from which events like the Industrial Revolution (and Imperialism) grew. The fact is that people in Europe had changed what was within (values, beliefs, etc.) and this changing of what was within hit the spot with the ultimate law of change giving Europe dominance over most of the world at the time. This again is another example of this law of change at work on a macro-level.

---

28 This event was narrated but not as an authentic Islamic hadith (i.e. just as recorded history) by many with various degrees of details, such as by Al-Jawzaqani in his work Al-Abateel (2/197), ibn Al-Jawzi in his work Alillal Al-Mutanahiya (2/388), Imam Al-Thahabi in his work Mizan Al-I'tidal (1/572), and many others.

PART FIVE
CONCLUSION

Take away from this that within you lies the power to achieve the seemingly impossible. Within you are emotions tied to a belief system that is dependent on your self-image to function correctly, and this self-image is dependent on your perception of life experiences. Within you are words that can either cripple or motivate you. Realize that you can influence which of destiny's paths you select and be comforted in knowing that while you can change your life with your freedom of choice, remember that everything that happens to you was destined by your Creator.

The law of attraction is merely a collection of psychological and social factors that affect behavior. Behavior is basically and predominantly a choice; a decision(s) subservient to free-will which is constantly under attack. But to believe the false philosophy attached to the law of attraction some of which has been proven false at the very core is dangerous. New age so called spiritual gurus have proven to be spiritual bankrupt and ignorant. They use facts to decorate false beliefs. You now know what components merit credibility and can distinguish them from the unrelated false conclusions. For example the idea that you can do and live whichever way you want and you will never be judged is morally bankrupt and promotes social oppression and injustice.

Use the knowledge within this book to change within yourself.

That is the true power of the freedom you have been given.

Rival tribes lost in ignorance and ongoing battles, who worshiped idols, changed what was within under the teachings of Islam and united as brothers and sisters to achieve the highest forms of moral and spiritual standards. Then they led the entire world scientifically to the point where they became the most powerful, respectable, and advanced society on earth at the time and for many centuries onward. This process only took twenty- three years! What worked for them will work for you. Keep in mind that it took twenty-three years to establish a society that changed the face of the earth and millions of people. You are only one individual and while you cannot control your environment, you can control yourself and reactions within this environment. What will be your condition twenty-three years from now? Seven years from now? A year from now? What about before you go to bed tonight?

Islam, with its Quran and Hadith, urges people to seek knowledge, to be positive, to have hope, to persevere, to set goals, and believe that they can achieve them, to trust in The Most Generous and Most Merciful, and pursue positive goals. It also teaches that both individuals and the community should focus on positive objectives, that education and self-improvement through seeking knowledge was divinely decreed upon us. One should work for this life as if he/she was going to live forever, and for the next life as if this day was his last. The Prophet (pbuh) often stressed the need to be optimistic and to avoid pessimistic and crippling thoughts. Within his teachings are endless treasures waiting to be discovered. Within your destiny are amazing unknowns waiting to be discovered based on the choices you make and the path you chose.

It is 1:30 A.M. I now find myself sipping the last portion of my soon-to-be-too-cold-to-drink cup of coffee and contemplating what would be an appropriate end to this short journey of light.

I have come to conclude that within what follows is immense value. I will refrain from commenting on the following Hadith and Quran verses for it has been passed down generations for over 1430 years without a change in a single letter. It is only appropriate that I leave it to you to extract what you see as vital to your own life.

Very often, people are not prepared to deal with the ultimate facts about life and how could they? Many of the ultimate truths about human life and history are so contradictory to what the new media-raised individuals have based their basic beliefs on. The truth is found so threatening at the deepest levels of one's preprogrammed psyche that they are violently rejected by one's basic survival instincts because they contradict the engineered social paradigm. Why not, when much of what they have come to accept as reality has been injected by parents, community, society, television, and now the internet (without going through even the least bit of objective thinking or evaluation). It was then accepted as standard and now lives in the psyche as one big smoke-screen.

The best method is often to ask the right questions in order to guide the individual towards the door. It is then their choice whether they open it or not.

RELEVANT QURAN AND HADITH

The following are a mix of Hadith and verses that will guide you about

The Law of Attraction and Islam

the best times for invocation and other related topics. An attempt was made not to overly "order" them because what may be of relevance to me concerning one issue, you may find of relevance to a different issue in your own life.

Finally, I feel it necessary to leave you with the confession that even though I often surrender to my benevolent tendencies, I am also a frequent victim of less than righteous impulses. Basically, I am no role model of the ideal Muslim man. So where can a frequent sinner such as myself find comfort and peace to reassure himself that in speaking of righteousness, he does not fall under the elusive shadow of hypocrisy? Among what follows are verses and Hadith that one can run to when seeking forgiveness for the decisions he knows he will regret some day. Some day when it is too late to ask for forgiveness, or do good.

Take from the following what you will. Each person will be touched differently by this nourishment for the heart and soul.

God said in the Quran:

> *"And when My servants ask you, [O Mohammed], concerning me—indeed I am near, I respond to the invocation of the supplicant when he calls upon me. So let them respond to Me that they may be [rightly] guided."*
>
> Quran 2:186

The Messenger of God (pbuh) said: "Our Lord, the Blessed and the Exalted, descends every night to the lowest heaven when one-third of the latter part of the night is left, and says: Who supplicates Me so that I may answer him? Who asks Me so that I may give to him? Who asks Me forgiveness so that I may forgive him?"[29]

The Prophet Mohammed (pbuh) said: "Whoever loves that he be

---

29 From the authentic narration in Sahih Muslim, Hadith number 758

granted more wealth and that his lease of life be prolonged then he should keep good relations with his Kith and kin."[30] (As in keeping close relations by giving time, being kind, and maintaining close relations with his parents, especially if they have reached old age, and other family members including siblings, grandparents' uncles etc.)

Another Hadith of interest to you for getting what you invocate is this:

The Prophet Mohammed (pbuh) said: "The nearest a servant comes to his Lord is when he is prostrating himself, so make supplication (in this state)."[31] (As in use this opportunity to ask for what you want)

The Prophet Mohammed (pbuh) said: "Invocations are not sent back (rejected) at the time between the call of prayer until the call for starting prayer"[32]

Allah's Messenger (pbuh) said, "Allah [God] said, 'O son of Adam! Spend, and I shall spend on you."[33]

There are also many Hadith that teach the following concerning the topic of invocation:

1. For those who are fasting, the time of breaking fast should be utilized for invocation because it is a time of acceptance for invocation. (Utilize the final hour before breaking fast time. It is of great benefit.)

2. Some of the things that deter wealth are sins, especially sins that are of injustice to others, not just yourself.

3. If you want to receive the full measure of wealth destined

---

30 From the authentic narration in Sahih Al-Bukhari, hadith number 5986
31 From the authentic narration in Sahih Muslim, hadith number 482
32 From the authentic narration in Sunan Abi Dawud, hadith number 521
33 From the authentic narration in Sahih Al-Bukhari, hadith number 5352

for you on a given day, you should insure you pray your morning prayer on time and in a Jamaa (with a group in a mosque if you are able to). It is a time when much of the blessings of the day are "released."

4. That one must avoid wearing cloth/jewelry, eating, or drinking anything that was obtained unjustly or purchased with impure money (money stolen or gained through cheating, lying, gambling...). These are all things that create a barrier which prevents the acceptance of invocation.

The Prophet (pbuh) said: "When Allah [God] decreed the Creation, He pledged Himself by writing in His book which is laid down with Him: My mercy prevails over my wrath."[34]

The Prophet (pbuh) said: "A man from among those who were before you was called to account. Nothing in the way of good was found for him, except that he used to have dealings with people and, being well-to-do, he would order his servants to let off (pardon and show leniency) the one in straitened circumstances [from repaying his debt]. He (the Prophet pbuh) said that Allah said, 'We are worthier than you of that (of being so generous). Let him off.'" (i.e. he was pardoned for generously pardoning people in difficult financial stress)[35]

In Surat az zumar in the Quran The Most Merciful said, in Aya Number 53–59:

"Say "O my servants who have transgressed against themselves [by sinning], do not despair of the mercy of Allah. Indeed,

---

[34] From the authentic narration in Sunan ibn majah, hadith number 4295
[35] From the authentic narrations in Sahih Al-Bukhari, hadith number 2077, and in Sahih Muslim, hadith number 1561

> Allah forgives all sins. Indeed, it is He who is The Most Forgiving, The Most Merciful." Return [in repentance] to your Lord and submit to Him before the punishment comes upon you, then you will not be helped. And follow the best of what was revealed to you [the Quran] from your Lord before the punishment comes upon you suddenly while you do not perceive, lest a soul should say [on the day of resurrection] "Oh, [how great is] my regret over what I neglected in regard to Allah and that I was among the mockers." Or [lest] it say, "If only Allah [God] had guided me, I would have been among the righteous." Or [lest] it say when it sees the punishment "If only I had another turn so I could be among the doers of good." But yes, there had come to you my verses, but you denied them and were arrogant, and you were among the disbelievers."
>
> Quran 39:53–59

In Surat Yunus, The Creator in the Quran says:

> "Say, "Who provides for you from the heavens and the earth? Or who controls hearing and sight and who brings the living out of the dead and brings the dead out of the living and who arranges [every] matter?" They will say, "Allah," so say "Then will you not be cautious (fearful) of him?" for that is Allah, your Lord, the truth. And what can be beyond the truth except error? So how are you averted? Thus, the word {i.e. decree} of your Lord has come into effect upon those who defiantly disobeyed—that they will not believe. Say, "Are there of your 'partners' any who begins creation and then repeats it?" Say, "Allah begins creation and then

repeats it, so how are you deluded?" Say, "Are there of your 'partners' any who guides to the truth?" Say, "Allah guides to the truth. So is He who guides to the truth more worthy to be followed or he who guides not unless he is guided? Then what is [wrong] with you—how do you judge?" Most of them follow not except assumption. Indeed, assumption avails not against the truth at all."

Quran 10:31–36

The Prophet (pbuh) narrating about his Lord I'm and said, "Allah ordered (the appointed angels over you) that the good and the bad deeds be written, and He then showed (the way) how (to write). If somebody intends to do a good deed and he does not do it, then Allah will write for him a full good deed (in his account with Him); and if he intends to do a good deed and actually did it, then Allah will write for him (in his account) with Him (its reward equal) from ten to seven hundred times to many more times: and if somebody intended to do a bad deed and he does not do it, then Allah will write a full good deed (in his account) with Him, and if he intended to do it (a bad deed) and actually did it, then Allah will write one bad deed (in his account)."[36]

The Prophet (pbuh) said: Allah the Almighty said:

"O son of Adam, so long as you call upon Me and ask of Me, I shall forgive you for what you have done, and I shall not mind. O son of Adam, were your sins to reach the clouds of the sky and were you then to ask forgiveness of Me, I would forgive you. O son of Adam, were you to come to Me with sins nearly as great as the earth and were you

---

36 From the authentic narration in Sahih Al-Bukhari, hadith number 6491

then to face Me, ascribing no partner to Me, I would bring you forgiveness nearly as great as it."[37]

> *Allah [God] said in the Quran, "No disaster strikes upon the earth or among and within yourselves except that it is in a "register" (preserved state, written in destiny) before we bring it into being—indeed, that for Allah is easy, in order that you not despair over what has eluded you and not exult in pride over what He has given you. Allah does not like everyone who is self- deluded and boastful-*
>
> Quran 57:22–23

RELEVANT QUOTES ON THE PROPHET MOHAMMED'S (PBUH) CHARACTER AND PERSONALITY.

Notice how non-Muslim scholars refer to him. The following quotes were freely available from http://muhammad.net on 15/9/2007:

> *"My choice of Muhammad to lead the list of the world's most influential persons may surprise some readers and may be questioned by others, but he was the only man in history who was supremely successful on both the religious and secular level."*
>
> **Michael H. Hart,** *The 100: A Ranking of the Most Influential Persons in History,* **New York: Hart Publishing Company, Inc., 1978,**
>
> p. 33.

---

37 From the narrations in the 40 hadith Qudsi, hadith number 34

"If greatness of purpose, smallness of means, and astounding results are the three criteria of human genius, who could dare to compare any great man in modern history with Muhammad? The most famous men created arms, laws, and empires only. They founded, if anything at all, no more than material powers which often crumbled away before their eyes. This man moved not only armies, legislations, empires, peoples and dynasties, but millions of men in one-third of the then inhabited world and more than that, he moved the altars, the gods, the religions, the ideas, the beliefs and souls... his forbearance in victory, his ambition, which was entirely devoted to one idea and in no manner striving for an empire his endless prayers, his mystic conversations with God, his death and his triumph after death all these attest not to an imposture but to a firm conviction which gave him the power to restore a dogma. This dogma was twofold, the unity of God and the immateriality of God the former telling what God is, the latter telling what God is not, the one overthrowing false gods with the sword, the other starting an idea with words. "Philosopher, orator, apostle, legislator, warrior, conqueror of ideas, restorer of rational dogmas, of a cult without images the founder of twenty terrestrial empires and of one spiritual empire, that is Muhammad. As regards all standards by which human greatness may be measured, we may well ask, is there any man greater than he?"

Lamartine, *Histoire de la Turquie*, Paris, 1854, Vol. II, pp. 276–277:

"It is not the propagation but the permanency of his religion

that deserves our wonder, the same pure and perfect impression which he engraved at Mecca and Medina is preserved, after the revolutions of twelve centuries by the Indian, the African, and the Turkish proselytes of the Koran... The Mahometans have uniformly withstood the temptation of reducing the object of their faith and devotion to a level with the senses and imagination of man. 'I believe in One God and Mahomet the Apostle of God' is the simple and invariable profession of Islam. The intellectual image of the Deity has never been degraded by any visible idol, the honours of the Prophet have never transgressed the measure of human virtue, and his living precepts have restrained the gratitude of his disciples within the bounds of reason and religion."

Edward Gibbon and Simon Ocklay, *History of the Saracen Empire*, London, 1870, p. 54.

"He was Caesar and Pope in one, but he was Pope without Pope's pretensions, Caesar without the legions of Caesar: without a standing army, without a bodyguard, without a palace, without a fixed revenue, if ever any man had the right to say that he ruled by the right divine, it was Mohammed, for he had all the power without its instruments and without its supports."

Bosworth Smith, *Mohammad and Mohammadanism*, London, 1874, p. 92.

"It is impossible for anyone who studies the life and character of the great Prophet of Arabia, who knows how he

taught and how he lived, to feel anything but reverence for that mighty Prophet, one of the great messengers of the Supreme. And although in what I put to you I shall say many things which may be familiar to many, yet I myself feel whenever I re-read them, a new way of admiration, a new sense of reverence for that mighty Arabian teacher."
Annie Besant, The Life and Teachings of Muhammad, Madras, 1932, p. 4.

"His readiness to undergo persecutions for his beliefs, the high moral character of the men who believed in him and looked up to him as leader, and the greatness of his ultimate achievement—all argue his fundamental integrity. To suppose Muhammad an impostor raises more problems than it solves. Moreover, none of the great figures of history is so poorly appreciated in the West as Muhammad."
W. Montgomery Watt, *Mohammad at Mecca,* Oxford, 1953, p. 52:

Encyclopedia Britannica confirms: "...a mass of detail in the early sources show that he was an honest and upright man who had gained the respect and loyalty of others who were likewise honest and upright men." (Vol. 12)

"I wanted to know the best of one who holds today's undisputed sway over the hearts of millions of mankind...I became more than convinced that it was not the sword that won a place for Islam in those days in the scheme of life. It was the rigid simplicity, the utter self-effacement of the Prophet, the scrupulous regard for his pledges, his intense devotion to his friends and followers, his intrepidity, his fearlessness, his absolute trust in God, and in his own mission. These and not the sword carried everything before them and surmounted every obstacle. When I closed the second volume (of the Prophet's biography), I was sorry there was not more for me to read of the great life." Mahatma Gandhi, speaking on the character of Muhammad, (pbuh) says in Yong India:

Thomas Carlyle in his Heroes and Hero-worship was simply amazed as to: "how one man could weld warring tribes and wandering Bedouins single-handedly into a most powerful and civilized nation in less than two decades."

Diwan Chand Sharma wrote: "Muhammad was the soul of kindness, and his influence was felt and never forgotten by those around him." (D.C. Sharma, The Prophets of the East, Calcutta, 1935, pp. 12)

Speaking on the aspect of equality before God in Islam, the famous poetess of India, Sarojinidaidu says: "It was the first religion that preached and practiced democracy; for, in the mosque, when the call for prayer is sounded and worshippers are gathered together, the democracy of Islam is embodied five times a day when the peasant and king kneel side by side and proclaim: 'God Alone is Great...' I have been struck over and over again by this indivisible unity of Islam that makes man instinctively a brother." (S. Naidu, Ideal of Islam, vide Speeches & Writings, Madras, 1918, p. 169)

"Muhammad, the Prophet of Islam," calls him the "Perfect model for human life." Prof. Ramakrishna Rao explains his point by saying: "The personality of Muhammad, it is most difficult to get into the whole truth of it. Only a glimpse of it I can catch. What a dramatic succession of picturesque scenes! There is Muhammad, the Prophet. There is Muhammad, the Warrior; Muhammad, the Businessman; Muhammad, the Statesman; Muhammad, the Orator; Muhammad, the Reformer; Muhammad, the Refuge of Orphans; Muhammad, the Protector of Slaves; Muhammad, the Emancipator of Women; Muhammad, the Judge; Muhammad, the Saint. All in all these magnificent roles, in all these departments of human activities, he is alike a hero." K. S. Ramakrishna Rao, an Indian professor of philosophy in his booklet

Robert Priffault concludes in his well-known book The Making of Humanity, "The debt of our science to the Arabs does not consist in startling discoveries or revolutionary theories. Science owes a great more to Arab culture; it owes is existence." The same writer says, "The Greeks systematized, generalized, and theorized but patient ways of investigation, the accumulation of positive knowledge, the minute methods of science, detailed and prolonged observation, and experimental inquiry were altogether alien to Greek temperament. What we call science arose in Europe as result of new methods of investigation, of the method of experiment, observation, measurement, and of the development of mathematics in form unknown to the Greeks. That spirit and these methods," concludes the same author, "were introduced into the European world by Arabs."

(The above quotes were retrieved from http://muhammad.net on 15 Nov 2007).

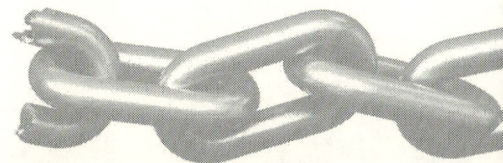

WORKS CITED

1. Al-Najar, Zaghlool. "The Scientifically Miraculous in the Quran and Sunna," (Title is in Arabic). Cassette recording in Arabic, part 1, tape 1. Egypt, Bedaia: 2001

2. Beaver, Diana. NLP for Lazy Learning. London: Vega, 2002.

3. Bennet, Paul. Abnormal and Clinical Psychology. Berkshire: Open University Press, 2006, second edition.

4. Blaszak, Nathan. How to Hypnotize Anyone without Getting Caught. ebook: www.ApplyHypnosis.com. USA: Life Tricks, 2006.

5. Blaszak, Nathan. (2004) Secret Book of Unconscious Gestures (eBook, www.ApplyHypnosis.com). USA: Life Tricks.

6. Blate, Michael. "The Natural Healer's Acupressure Handbook," Basic G-Jo, Volume 1. Florida: Falkynor Books, 1983, special expanded ed.

7. Branan, Nicole. "Unconscious Decisions," Scientific American Mind, August, September, Vol. 19, no.4.8 (August/September 2008).

8. Byrne, Rhonda (Producer) and Drew Heriot (Director). The Secret (motion picture). Melbourne: Prime Time Productions, 2006.

9. Cheung, William. How to Develop Chi Power, ed. by Mike Lee. California: Ohara Publications, Inc., 1996, 11th printing.

10. DiMatteo, M. Robin and Howard S. Friedman. Social Psychology and Medicine. Massachusetts: Oelgeschlager, Gunn, and Hain Publishers Inc., 1982 printed in West Germany.

11. Dong, Paul and Thomas Raffil. Empty Force. Dorset: Element Books Limited, 1996.

12. Gladwell, Malcolm. Blink. London: Penguin Group, 2005.

13. Godefroy, Christian H. Mind Powers How to Use and Control Your Unlimited Potential. eBook: Laffont, Robert. http://www.trans4mind.com/godefroy/

14. Griffin, Edward G. The Hidden Agenda for World Government (documentary/video interview). Interview with Norman Dodd, conducted by G. Edward Griffin in 1982. California: Quantum Communications, 1982.(For more information, contact American Media, P.O. box 4646, Westlake Village, CA 91359 phone (800) 282873)

15. Hawking, Stephen. A Brief History of Time. New York: Bantam Books, 1998, 10th ed.

16. Hogan, Craig J. The Little Book of the Big Bang. New York: Copernicus, 1998.

17. Hopper, Carolyn H. Practicing College Learning Strategies. New York: Patricia A. Coryell, 4th ed., Houghton Miffin Co., 2007.

18. Wordpress, "Moral Decision-Making and the Ventromedial Prefrontal Cortex," http://phineasgage. wordpress.com/2007/03/23/moral-decision-making-and-the-ventromedial-prefrontal-cortex/ (accessed March 23, 2003).

19. La Tourrete, John M. Beginner's Secrets to Poison Hands and Nerve Strikes, (Live recording of two-hour seminar). Orlando: Warrior Publications, 1998.

20. Lee, Bruce. Tao of Jeet Kune Do. California: Ohara Publications Inc., 1975, 44th printing, 1998.

21. Lieberman, David J. Get Anyone to Do Anything. New York: St. Martin's Griffin, 2000.

22. Lindstrom, Martin. Buy ology. New York: Doubleday, 2008.

23. Melville, Kate. "Liar, Liar, Your Prefrontal Cortex Is on Fire," http://www.scienceagogo.com/news/20050904005107datatruncsys.shtml (accessed Nov. 1, 2008).

24. Mcgills,Ormond.Professional Stage Hypnotism. California: Westwood Publishing Co., 1977.

25. Morris, Glenn. Path Notes of an American Ninja Master. California: North Atlantic Books, 1993.

26. Nierenberg, Gerard I. and Henry H. Calero. How to Read a Person Like a Book. U.S.A.: Barnes & Noble, Inc., 1994.

27. Peck, M. Scott. Further along the Road Less Traveled. New York: Simon & Schuster, 1993.

28. Ramakrishna Rao, K. S. Mohammed the Prophet, http://www.nz-muslim.net/viewarticle-7.html (accessed Nov. 2008, repr. Islam and Modern Age).

29. Robbins, Anthony. Awaken the Giant Within. New York: Free Press, 2003.

30. Schwartz, Barry. "When Words Decide," Scientific American Mind, August/September 2007, Vol. 18, no. 4, 37–43.

31. How to Use Sports Psychology, "Professional Athletes Using Hypnosis to Enhance Mental Toughness and Peak Performance," by (Jack Singer), http://www. howtousesportspsychology.com/Professional-Athletes- Using-Hypnosis.html (accessed April 11, 2008).

32. Tarbuck, Edward J. and Frederik K.Lutgens. Earth: an Introduction to Physical Geology, ed. by Patrick Lynch. New Jersey: Prentice Hall, 2002, seventh edition.

33. Golfnosis, "Visualization," http://www.golfnosis.com/visualization.html (accessed November 2008).

34. Walker, A. Flane and Richard C. Bauer. The Ancient Art of Life and Death: The Book of Dim Mak. Colorado: Paladin Press, 2002.

35. Weinberg, George. The Heart of Psychotherapy. New York: St. Martin's Griffin, 1996, first St. Martin's Griffin ed.

36. http://quran.muslim-web.com Retrieved august 2009

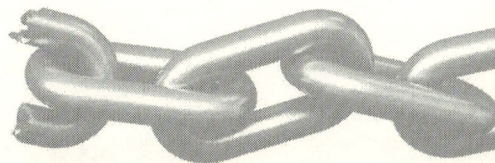

Made in the USA
Las Vegas, NV
24 June 2023